MW00791954

HOUSTON REAL ESTATE INVESTORS DREAM TEAM

Behind the Scenes Look at Investing in Houston from Top Real Estate Pros

Copyright © 2015 Ainsley & Allen Publishing,
a division of Authority Media Group, LLC

All rights reserved. No portion of this book may be reproduced--mechanically, electronically, or by any other means without the expressed written permission of the authors except as provided by the United States of America copyright law.

Published by Ainsley & Allen Publishing, a division of Authority Media Group, LLC
Houston, TX

ISBN-13: 978-0692477212 (Ainsley & Allen Publishing)

The Publisher has strived to be as accurate and complete as possible in the creation of this book.

This book is not intended for use as a source of legal, business, accounting or financial advice. All readers are advised to seek services of competent professionals in legal, business, accounting, and financial fields.

In practical advice books, like anything else in life, there are no guarantees of income made. Readers are cautioned to rely on their own judgment about their individual circumstances and to act accordingly.

While all attempts have been made to verify information provided in this publication, the Publisher assumes no responsibility for errors, omissions, or contrary interpretation of the subject matter herein. Any perceived slights of specific persons, peoples, or organizations are unintentional.

HOUSTON REAL ESTATE INVESTORS DREAM TEAM

Behind the Scenes Look at Investing in
Houston from Top Real Estate Pros

Brant Phillips
Michael Plaks
Shelly Walzel
Nick Koren
Steven S. Newsom
Blake A. Yarborough
H. Quincy Long
David Lee Durr
Chris Adkins
Sal Ortiz
Rhonda Conchola
C. Jerry Ta
Thuy T. Vo

CONTENTS

INTRODUCTION

While it is tempting to try to manage all of the details of real estate investing on your own, the DIY approach is a costly mistake. Building a team of knowledgeable professionals can make your life easier and allow you to focus on running your business. Whether you are buying your first property or expanding your investment empire, the right professionals can help you locate the best deals, secure the financing your need to purchase and then manage your income and the properties themselves.

Building your real estate investment portfolio will be easier when you accumulate a team of advisors to turn to who will look out for your interests and help you as you navigate your way through a transaction. From a savvy and connected acquisition team that can give you advance notice of new properties to the legal and finance teams you'll need to make the deals happen, buying and selling is stress free if you have expert help. Once you've added a property to your portfolio, a management team can help you with the day to day operations and make sure your business runs worry free.

Smart investors recognize that each member of their team as not a cost to their business, but rather a source of substantially increased profits.

6 Essential Team Members You Will Need on Your Side When You Invest in Houston Real Estate

Acquisition & Sales: If you are interested in rehabbing distressed properties or in acquiring foreclosure or short sale properties, relationships with trusted and knowledgeable professionals are essential. Having active professionals working to find you properties and opportunities puts you in the driver's seat. Being able to consider a diverse group of properties at any given time gives you the flexibility you need to make the best choices for your business, on your terms.

Your team should include the best, most connected real estate broker, realtors, and wholesalers to help you get fast notice when ideal properties come onto the market. Everyday, great investment properties are listed on the MLS; the best are put under contract within hours. Others may never even make it into the MLS because a savvy, connected investor snaps them up before they become public knowledge.

When it's time to sell an investment property, smart investors turn to the real estate broker / agent that understand what it takes to market and sell or lease their property quickly and at the best price to match their investment goals.

Renovation and Construction: A team that can step in and quickly rehab or turnover a property between tenants can cut your down time and make sure your units and homes are ready to show. A home stager can help you maximize the curb appeal and presence of each property and make sure you get the best rental rate possible for your units.

Using the same company repeatedly allows you to secure a better deal on each project you do. You'll also find you get the prime spots on the schedule if you use a contractor or renovation team on a regular basis. If you are renovating multiple units at the same time, speed and attention is a must; the longer your units sit empty during repairs, the less money you'll make on them.

Investors specializing in higher end renovations understand the value and increased profit by using the services of a home staging professional to put the finishing touches that can more than pay for itself as a result of higher price and quicker sale.

Legal: A knowledgeable real estate attorney is not only important to have when buying and selling individual properties, but can help protect your entire investment empire, as well as your personal assets. There are many variables involved in deciding the best legal structure for your business, especially if there are partners involved. Having the right attorney that understands the ins and outs of buying and selling real estate is crucial for your business.

Finance: Investing requires money – from the funds you'll need to put down to purchase a property to the portion you'll finance. Your investment and equity team can provide the connections and confidence that funds are available when you need them.

Smart successful investors understand that it's not the money you have it's the money you have access to that will allow them to take advantage of the best investment opportunities.

If you finance a portion or all of your properties, relationships with mortgage professionals; hard money lenders and private money sources are a must. From creating and maintaining an excellent relationship with a preferred traditional lender to more creative financing options will allow you to get the funds you need, when you need them.

Property Management: The unsung heroes of the real estate investment business, a good property manager can save you time, money and headaches by coping with tenants, repairs and issues that arise with your individual properties. Tenant issues can leech both your profits and your enthusiasm and having an extra layer between you and your renters means you won't have to cope with squabbles, 2am phone calls or the stress that comes with managing people, not houses.

Accounting: From handling the day-to-day bookkeeping that every business must deal with to ensuring that you are in compliance with the unique tax implications that come with real estate investments, your bookkeeper and accounting professional is a source of valuable data that allows you to make the right buying, selling and management decisions at the right time; decisions that can mean the difference between profit and loss for your business.

Mentor: Finding the right players for each part of your real estate investment team will reduce your stress and increase your profitability. One the most important members of your team can be your Mentor. In fact, your mentor may be able to help you make the right decisions when choosing many of the other members of your team.

Your mentor should be an educator and advocate for your success. Someone that has been where you want to be; someone that not only understands but also empathizes with the obstacles and challenges you will face along your journey.

A mentor will be there to help you overcome these obstacles and help you celebrate successes. Most successful real estate investors will tell you that their mentor was an integral part of their success.

As a Real Estate Mentor myself, I'm extremely proud to be able to introduce you to this team of smart folks that are true educators and advocates for your investing success. I've worked closely with each of these professionals in my own business of buying, flipping, repairing, and leasing properties. I know that each of their contributions to this important book will help a great many investors.

We are living in one of the most exciting times for investing in the Houston housing market – I firmly believe you'll find the information on the following pages can help you make your dreams a reality – Brant Phillips.

INVESTMENT AND CONSTRUCTION ADVISOR

Brant Phillips is the founder of Invest Home Pro, a real estate investment, construction, and education company in Houston, Texas

As one of Houston's most trusted and experienced advisors in the real estate investment market, Brant has been involved in close to a thousand real estate rehabs, either as his own projects or in a consulting role.

Brant helps people successfully invest in residential real estate by teaching them how to master all aspects of investing. His training helps investors learn how to analyze deals, raise capital, manage renovation projects, as well as many other aspects of real estate investing. He teaches by showing them systems that he has put together and used to successfully build his own real estate investment portfolio.

Brant's strategies can be utilized for investors to buy, fix, flip or rent residential homes in any market.

Whether an investor wants to take charge of his own project, or wants to hand over the keys to have the work done, Invest Home Pro meets the needs of both markets.

Conversation with Brant Phillips

As a real estate investor and advisor, you always have a great team behind you making sure everything comes together. Many people see you as the conductor of a symphony. You're not the guy playing the violin, the drums, or the oboe, you're the one directing them to create a successful outcome.

Would it be accurate to say that you help people that want to be investors find the right team to be successful?

Brant Phillips: Yes, absolutely. With my coaching students, we work to overcome the fears that they have. It's the fear or the concern that they're not going to have either enough time to invest, or the financial fear that they're not going to have the capital to invest.

So, my job as a coach and as an educator is to help them overcome those fears.

And the funny thing is that a lot of those fears they have are really false beliefs. Because when you learn the power of creating a team, you understand that although there is time that's required to build a successful real estate investing business, it doesn't necessarily need to be your time. When you build the right team, you're able to leverage other people's skillsets, their resources, and their time to help you really grow your investment portfolio and grow your investment business.

The critical piece here, and this is what I work on with my students, is making sure that they're finding the right people for their team. You hit the nail on the head – it's like a symphony conductor – coordinating people and bringing in the right people that are going to be the right fit to achieve the ultimate goal for your real estate investment business.

Many people do not know much about real estate investors other than what they see on TV reality shows. It seems to be the case in most of these real estate investment shows that the houses investors buy are in much worse condition than the investor originally thought. So is that the norm, or is that the exception that makes good TV?

Brant Phillips: That's funny you mentioned that because I was actually just writing an email today about that. Real estate investing is not typically as interesting as many of those TV shows, so they have to create those scenarios.

Of course, there are some unknowns whenever you invest, especially when you're first starting out and you're going it alone without a coach or a mentor and don't have any experience.

Those homes that are all beat up and the "ugly houses" seem much more overwhelming than what they really are. If you have a team of service individuals, contractors, or an inspector that can walk you through and explain, 'No, this is really bad," or "No, this isn't bad at all – that can be easily fixed," it can help you avoid surprises and make better decisions on which properties to purchase.

You've worked with people that have a lot of different levels of experience with investing. They range from people that have been doing this for years and understand the power of a team, to people that are just getting started and really have no idea where to begin.

You can separate the types of clients you work with into two groups.

There are people that want to be real estate entrepreneurs. They thrive on what they see on the TV and that's what they want to do. They want to replace their job. They're stuck in the corporate rat race or they are in a career that they don't enjoy and they really have a calling to real estate. They want to make that what they do when they get up every day.

Then you have people that are happy with their careers, but they're looking for an alternative to traditional stocks and mutual funds as ways to build wealth and build retirement. They aren't necessarily looking to have anything to do with the day-to-day operations of real estate, but are more interested in using it as an investment vehicle.

Which type of client do you work with the most that you feel you're really successful at helping?

Brant Phillips: Most of our work is with the full-time executive, Corporate America-type of individual or small business owner that is interested in real estate and they're looking to grow their net worth, grow their wealth, and maybe increase cash flow with some rental properties.

But they don't necessarily want to leave their job and be a full-time real estate entrepreneur. They're just looking to grow their net worth. Sometimes, some of them just have some extra capital to invest and they've maybe read a few books or went to a seminar and they know the benefits and the upside of successfully and wisely investing in real estate.

That's the core of who we work with and who we serve. The 80/20 rule probably applies here as that's 80% of our clientele.

Then there is the 20% who come in focused and they're determined that they want to do this full-time. They want to leave their job, or want to close their business, or get to a point where they can just let their business run as a self-sustaining business and focus more on real estate and make that their primary income source.

That's the smaller portion of our clientele, but I can relate to both sides. When I first got started, I was in Corporate America and I was working a job that I, to be quite honest, disliked a great deal. I was determined to leave and become a full-time real estate entrepreneur. So I can see both sides of the coin and work with both.

We definitely work with both types to tailor and create a game plan that works to achieve their ultimate goal.

Some people come into real estate investing just to get their feet wet and dabble with it a little bit. However, some of them discover that they really, really like it and end up transitioning and working a one-year, two-year or five-year plan to eventually leave their business.

Another common scenario is they're setting themselves up for after they retire, so that they'll have something to do that they enjoy doing which also makes money at the same time.

People that have full-time jobs and are looking to real estate to grow their wealth may have concerns about the amount of time and money needed. They think, "I don't have the time to tear up sheetrock and hammer through windows and manage contractors."

When people are looking for investment strategies or growing wealth, traditionally they think about stocks or mutual funds. They read the paper and watch somebody on TV that tells them, "Here's what hot. Here's what's not." They pick up the phone or log onto their computer and make a decision. That's the extent of their involvement.

Do a lot of your clients come to you with that perception, or maybe misconception, that to use real estate to build wealth requires a great deal of their time?

Brant Phillips: Yes, definitely. That's the big one. A lot of people come into real estate and they put a lot of pressure on themselves and much of it turns out to be an unnecessary and not beneficial.

One of the pressures is that this is going to take a lot of time. It is true that if done incorrectly, it can take a great amount of time to fix it.

One of the first things I do with the students I work with to alleviate a lot of that pressure is by convincing them to start with just one. All we need to focus on right now is that first deal. And then, in order to work on that first deal, let's find the first team member and then the second team member and the third team member.

Building your team and Building your business by taking one deal at a time, one step at a time. It's similar to a marathon, which is 26 miles, but it starts with just one step. And that's all we focus on.

We take one deal at a time and one step at a time. During this process, I determine what their goals are.

The time involved can be spread out or you can speed up that process. You can also slow it down. The thing is that there's a lot of false pressure that people put on themselves, because this is not a race. There's no clock when you begin real estate investing. It's much more important to be comprehensive and diligent and patient to find the right deal and the right team member. To put together the right team is one step at a time.

So time is one of those preconceived fears that people have that becomes a non-issue when you do this wisely and you put together your business plan properly.

A lot of people compare investing in real estate to investing in stocks and mutual funds. What many people don't consider is that when investing in a stock you have a team there. You're not deciding what to buy, going down to the NASDAQ trading floor, jumping into the pit and making your trades and turning them in.

You have a team that does those things, but you only have one person to contact and that's your broker.

You seem to play the role of the stockbroker in real estate investing. When someone wants to invest in real estate, they don't need to go out and swing the hammer. You put all the pieces together so they just have one place they need to go to, similar to what a stockbroker would do, correct?

Brant Phillips: Yes, exactly.

When it comes to building your team, there are essentially three circles of team members that you're going to need.

First, you need to establish your inner circle. This is going to include partners, consultants, mentors, and coaches. They're going to guide you and direct you on some of the critical decisions you'll be making, and essentially help you to build the other two circles of your team.

Next, you're going to create a support circle. The support circle is critical and includes people such as your real estate agent, your banker, and your private lenders. It also includes your accountants, attorneys, property managers, contractors, etc. These people support you logistically in your business.

Then, finally you've got the outer circle, which is comprised of your service-type professionals. These include your appraisers, inspectors, the title company, and perhaps a landscaper.

It really does require these three circles - three different layers of team members. But it starts with that inner circle which provides good help and support in coaching to build up your plan.

Then you grow the next layer of your team, which is the professional people in this industry that you can go to and rely on their time and energy and experience to help you grow your business.

No matter what people do, you can't buy more than 24 hours in a day to do it yourself. But you can certainly leverage the time of other people to get things done. Each person brings with them their own specialty and expertise.

Another perceived obstacle to real estate investing is money. One thing that might surprise a lot of people is that many real estate investors don't necessarily start out with a lot of money. The reality is that people don't have to have a lot or any cash for that matter to buy a house and make this work. There are a lot of options for leveraging other people's money in the same way that they would leverage other people's time.

What do you tell your clients that don't have a lot of cash?

Brant Phillips: That's one of the things that attracted me to real estate investing and I see that it attracts a lot of other people. One thing that brings people to real estate is they've heard that there is the possibility of real estate offering creative financing opportunities.

So, when I started in real estate, my wife and I were in a position where we had just paid off our student loans and we had paid off all of our other debts. We had a baby and paid off the doctor bills from that. We were doing the Dave Ramsey thing. We were debt free.

At that time, I knew that the Corporate America path was not something I wanted to pursue. I was attracted to real estate because of the possibilities that I had read about in some books of being able to have this creative financing and do "no money down" deals.

While I've invested a lot of cash over the years into real estate, I can tell you that a majority of the deals I've done have been without any money down.

So that's the thing. Whenever you dive into this business, you can see that real estate does provide a lot of opportunities to make deals and purchase houses without putting money down. There's a philosophy that we use in real estate that is real estate should put money into your pocket, rather than take it out.

With that being said, there are some people coming into real estate who specifically have money and they have capital that they want to invest. Real estate is a great place to make that investment and make great returns when invested wisely.

In addition, there are opportunities where you can get rates of return that you can't find anywhere else because there are opportunities to do deals with no money out of pocket, so your rates of return are infinite.

It is a common misconception among people that they have to have a lot of money to get started in real estate. And it's just not true.

I tell a story about when I actually got my first home. My wife and I had gotten to that place where we had paid off all of our debt and student loans. But we didn't have any money in the bank.

I don't want to make it sound like we were on the streets, but we were just living very conservatively and had paid everything off and we had great credit. We used our credit scores to actually buy our first investment property using a credit card. That's not something I advise, but it's what we did. I leveraged our good credit to buy my very first property without any money out of pocket.

So I've seen both sides. I went on to buy dozens and dozens of houses over the next several years, mainly rental properties at that time, without any money out of pocket.

Now occasionally, when we have capital to invest, we do invest that capital. So there are opportunities in real estate where you can do deals with no money down or you can choose to invest your capital into your real estate deals. Either way is possible. People just come in with the misconception that only one way is possible, and that's certainly not the case.

Right. And there is obviously the fear people have about losing their money. They wonder if they should jump into this not knowing what they're doing.

What is it that you think creates the perception some people have that investing in real estate is scary, or it's scarier than just putting their money into a mutual fund or a stock?

Brant Phillips: I think that the fear of the unknown, like anything that you're not educated about or fully aware of what the consequences are, can be very strong. I think that's where a lot of that fear comes from. It's just a lack of education or a lack of experience.

Generally, as you increase your education, you increase your experience and that fear can actually begin to turn into excitement. Physiologically in our bodies, the funny thing is that the physiological response in our bodies to fear is exactly the same as to excitement. With fear, we stop breathing and things slow down and we panic a little bit. But when you're excited you breathe.

People come to me and say, "I can't imagine how you know everything you know about real estate. The things that you do and some of the deals that you do, the renovations that you do, spending $50,000 to $200,000 on a renovation or building a home and doing new development and things like that. I don't know how you put all this together."

I explain that I started out like all investors start out - with zero knowledge and zero experience. And I'd still have that same type of fear if I had to step into the shoes of some of my clients' professions or businesses. It would be very scary for me, at least in the beginning, not having the same knowledge and experience that they have.

I think it's just one of those things that it's normal. Part of the process is understanding that there is going to be some fear, which is just really not knowing certain things, in the beginning.

But as you begin to educate yourself and gain experience, learn from the experiences of others and become educated by your team members, that fear will subside and turn to excitement.

That's when it gets really fun - when you see all the upside that's in real estate and the enormous amounts of wealth and money that can be made. The fear will begin to subside when you find yourself where you can visualize and see the benefits and some of the success that you can have by doing real estate deals.

The way that you help people goes beyond just being a service provider. In that role of mentor, you've probably seen several people actually go through those stages – from the stage of the unknown and fear, to the stage of overcoming that fear and then the stage of actually achieving that first success.

Can you give an example of a situation where you worked with a client who went from the fear, the unknown, to where they actually made that transition from "I'm going to be an investor" to "I am an investor"?

Brant Phillips: I'll tell you about one of my students named Keith who is in the Dallas, Texas area.

I was working with him and mentoring him. In my program, we go through at least a thirty or sixty day process just to build a foundational level of knowledge.

We go through some training and the process of building a team, starting out slowly. Creating some deal flow. Learning how to evaluate deals and estimate repairs and put together financing. Basically, I take them through the fundamentals of real estate investing before they start.

About two months into this process, Keith hit a little bit of a mental roadblock, which is pretty typical. He was a little tired and started thinking, “Maybe this isn’t for me. Maybe I shouldn’t be doing this. Maybe I should just go back to focus on my job and what I was doing before.”

And Keith was making a transition to go full time as a real estate investor.

He wanted to give up because of the fear of the unknown and some of the doubt that crept in.

As a coach, I get the most enjoyment from some of these times when people are going through this “valley” or these trying times. So I just kept plugging away with Keith and encouraging him to keep his head up. To keep pushing forward and really keeping him focused on the possibilities of why he got into real estate. Keith was looking to flip houses. That was his goal – to flip five to ten houses a year.

He stayed on the path. He didn’t give up. About a week after that, he got his first deal under contract. Long story short, two months later, he had purchased it, renovated it and put it on the market a few days before Thanksgiving and received a full price offer in less than 7 days.

He had three or four days after he listed the property where he really wasn’t getting any showings and he thought, “What’s going on here?” I told him it’s just the holidays. We made a couple of tweaks with his listing and added some pictures. I told him to be calm, be still and watch what happens the next week.

The following week on Monday, he had multiple offers. He sold that house and made about $35,000. His confidence completely changed to the point where I got two more calls from him over the next couple of months.

One call was, “Hey, I’ve got my other deal.” He needed no help. No assistance to analyze it or talk about the rehab.

Then I got another call from him saying, "Hey, guess what? I put the house on the market. I have multiple offers. Here's the one I'm going to accept and here's why." And he went into coaching me and telling me about the whole process and how it went.

So that was one of those situations where Keith went from inexperienced, having fear, and having doubt to just continuing to plug away doing some of the fundamental activities that successful investors do.

And he kept plugging away and it was a shift. It was like night and day when he turned from having doubts in himself, to where he was like, "I've got this. I've already got my next deal under contract. I'm about to flip it and I'm moving on to the next one."

And that's how it plays out when people stay committed and focused. And he built a great team. I'm not in the Dallas area, so I have never been up there to work with him in person in Dallas or nor have I met any of his contractors or lenders or anything like that. He did this all by himself, by following a proven process and some fundamentals that we know work.

It's amazing the change that occurs in someone's mindset once people make that transition from "I'm going to be" or "I want to be" to "I am."

Brant Phillips: Definitely.

What led you to create this business that allows you to help investors take that journey and make that transition?

Brant Phillips: The funny thing that happened was I started transitioning from Corporate America to becoming a real estate investor and I really identified myself as a real estate investor. Being a full-time real estate investor.

I started going out and doing deals and having success. I began sharing that with other people and I started getting a lot of messages through social media, emails and phone calls from people of how I was inspiring them to take action.

I really started thinking about how my life had changed and how my financial situation had changed and how everything had improved. It also led me to thinking back to when I had felt stuck. When I had those feelings of fear and doubt and worry while I was working my corporate job.

The funny thing is the more I've transitioned to being a coach, I find it's so much more rewarding to me whenever I'm able to help people who are stuck. They're in that corporate job or they're fearful of not having enough money to retire or they need extra cash flow. To help those people has become more rewarding for me than the deals I actually do.

Of course, I'm still active. I'm still doing a lot of real estate, as much as I've ever done. Unlike a lot of the other real estate gurus, I'm an investor first.

But to answer the question of what led me to teach and help others and coach and mentor – it's the excitement that comes whenever I am able to help people achieve their dreams and success and leave their job. Or just build their retirement monies.

It's so much more rewarding to me than doing it myself. It's very similar to teaching my daughter to ride her bike. When she learned and when she took that first ride on her own, it was so much more rewarding to watch my daughter ride a bike than it is for me to get on my own bike and ride.

So I think it's been the progression of learning how to do it and then leading and teaching other people how to do it. That's what I encourage my students to do as well.

Once you learn it, go out and teach others and inspire others. Because it's so much more rewarding and there are ancillary benefits that come along with it as well, such as some of the relationships and deals and partnerships that come about from helping other people are really incredible.

Well, this is an industry where good news travels fast and bad news travels faster.

You have a great reputation as someone that does things the right way without taking shortcuts. People look to you as a trusted advisor. It's about building a real business and building a solid business. That's what people come to you for – to get real answers in a world where a lot of easy answers are what's being sold.

How can people find out more about Brant Phillips and what you're doing and how to get involved with what you're doing?

Brant Phillips: The easiest way is to go to my website, which is www.BrantPhillips.com.

Also check out www.InvestHomePro.com and www.F7XFactor.com for more details.

About Brant Phillips

Brant is a full-time real estate investor, business owner, entrepreneur, author and speaker. He has been featured on Fox News, he hosts local seminars, and he is even being considered to star in one of those "Flipping Houses" TV shows.

Brant is a proverbial 'rags to riches' story. While living in an apartment and having no money, was able to purchase his first investment property on a credit card! He went on to buy ten properties that same year with no money down. A few years later, he has rehabbed hundreds of homes, owns a portfolio of rental properties worth millions, and routinely flips houses for fast cash.

Brant is a former police officer who prides himself on integrity and serving others. He is a husband and father of four and enjoys helping and teaching people to experience the freedom and success he has achieved through successfully investing in real estate.

Business Name: Invest Home Pro

Websites: www.BrantPhillips.com and www.InvestHomePro.com

Facebook: www.Facebook.com/BrantAPhillips

YouTube: www.YouTube.com/Brant5300

F7XFactor:	www.F7XFactor.com
Breakthrough at the Beach:	www.BreakthroughAtTheBeach.com

MICHAEL PLAKS

TAX ACCOUNTANT

As a specialist in real estate transactions, tax accountant Michael Plaks provides services that are one of the most critical pieces of running a real estate investment business.

Many people working in the real estate realm do not understand the distinctions the IRS makes between people who hold rental properties and those who flip or wholesale properties. As an educator, in addition to helping with the financial aspects of the business, Michael teaches his clients the critical differences between what the IRS considers to be two separate businesses. He also explains the two types of income that result from these two real estate businesses.

Michael's advice is helping investors not only follow the letter of the law and stay out of trouble with the IRS, but also helping them save money they might otherwise lose.

Conversation with Michael Plaks

People don't like to think about taxes and often wait until a week before taxes are due to get everything together for their tax return.

What do you see as the biggest mistake that real estate investors are making when it comes to their tax situation?

Michael Plaks: The biggest mistake probably is assuming that this is a simple task that takes very little effort and can be done, like you said, a week before April 15th. Let's slap together a few numbers, have the computer come up with what you owe to Uncle Sam, and then move on with your business without giving any more thought to this unpleasant task. But this is not how it works.

A lot of people just do checkbook accounting for their own personal lives. As long as there's money in the bank, I'm doing my bookkeeping.

Michael Plaks: Certainly. As an example, if you have a simple business, let's say you are a Realtor or a handyman or selling something on eBay, then bookkeeping and taxes would be very simple. You can count everything that you put into your bank account as your income and everything that you paid out of your account as expenses. One minus the other is the resulting profit. Then you calculate taxes on that profit. It's very simple.

Unfortunately, real estate tax calculations have nothing to do with that simplicity.

Yes. Unfortunately, I think a lot of people do it that way. That's why it's important, when people are choosing a tax professional, that they choose someone that is not just kind of familiar, but someone that is intimately familiar with real estate finance and taxes, as you are. You pretty much are laser-focused on helping investors in the real estate area, specifically, real estate investors – people that flip houses and people that are landlords.

It is important to note the difference between those two, because how they set up their business and structure things can have a dramatic impact on their bottom line.

You have clients that are house flippers and then you have clients that are buying and holding. Those are the primary groups that people can identify themselves with in real estate.

What is the big difference between those two groups, and what kind of decisions does someone need to make, depending on which one of those camps they put themselves in?

Michael Plaks: This is a perfect question that betrays the fact that you are intimately familiar with the real estate business yourself.

When we talk about bookkeeping and taxes, we are looking at how the IRS distinguishes between two types of real estate businesses.

The difficulty is for a new investor to understand this distinction. When we go to a networking event, we introduce ourselves as a 'real estate investor.' That implies we're buying real estate, and we sell it or rent it out. For a businessperson, for an investor, that's one type of business.

The IRS, however, draws a line and says these are *two distinct businesses, not one.*

One is being a landlord renting property out. Everything else is the other type – a resale type of business, where you buy and sell, including flippers, wholesalers, builders, and all other forms of real estate businesses.

It's very difficult for an investor who is not certain about his business plan, his exit strategy, and the focus of his real estate business, to think not in terms of "I am an investor," but in terms of "I'm running a business which actually is two separate businesses." One will be the rental side: buy, fix and hold. The other will be the resale side: buy, fix and sell.

The reason why it's so important to separate the two, is because when you are trying to put it on IRS forms, you will find two different sets of Federal forms and two different sets of tax rules that apply to them.

See, the rent that you collect from a tenant and a down payment that you collect from a person who is buying your flip, they may be the exact same amount of money, but they are taxed completely differently and go on different IRS forms.

If you attempt to add them together, which would be the simple commonsense way of looking at money as a business person, you'd say, "Let's add up all of that and call it income." No, you cannot combine them. There is no IRS form to report it this way. At the end of the day, you will have to treat them differently.

I use an analogy to bring this point home. When you get into a car, you either sit in the driver's seat or a passenger seat, not both. Sometimes you drive, and at other times you are a passenger. Always one or the other. But never both at the same time. Likewise, with each investment property, you're either a landlord or a flipper, but not both.

That's an important distinction that a lot of people miss – a person that buys and sells properties, and a person that holds properties to rent, are really in two very, very different businesses in the eyes of the IRS.

So, when someone is setting up the business, you talk about how important it is to understand their exit strategy up front.

What are some of the things that they would need to consider when setting up the business? For instance, when would someone set up an LLC, and when would someone want to set up a corporation? How does this decision impact their tax liabilities and outcomes?

Michael Plaks: You just opened a very important discussion, because whenever you're building the structure for a new company, there are two, or even three, different considerations.

The first two are obvious: legal protection and taxes. There is a third angle on that: control of the business when multiple people are involved, which is a major consideration, different from legal liability and taxes. Who makes the decisions, what happens when roles change or when one partner wants out, and so on. These issues can get very complicated and are always case-by-case.

That said, when we focus on the two universal concerns - legal protection and taxes - those two considerations are not always aligned, and they might dictate different approaches.

Now, talking about LLCs and business entities, we have to start from what we discussed a few minutes ago: the two very different types of real estate businesses. One is renting or landlording. The other is the resale business, which includes flipping.

The important thing to remember is that they have to be separated. So if you are planning the structure and creating an LLC or any other type of entity, you have to create different setups for these two businesses. They should not be combined together. That's number one.

If we tackle the rental business first, on the rental side, you cannot extract any tax advantages by creating an entity. Well, attorneys and CPAs and accountants, when we say never, there is always some exception to the general rule. But, as a general rule, you will not derive tax benefits from creating an entity for rentals.

In other words, if you are a landlord, whether you have an LLC or you don't have an LLC, you will pay the exact same amount of taxes at the end of the day. So, the reason to form an LLC when you are a landlord will be strictly legal protection, and that is an attorney's area.

From my perspective, when a new investor comes, and they are planning to buy and hold rentals, and they ask what they need for taxation purposes, I tell them go ask your attorney for legal protection recommendations. Somebody who also specializes in real estate, like Steve Newsom. The attorney will give them direction from legal protection perspective.

I will tell these new investors that on my side, as far as tax benefits go, entities do not matter for landlords. You cannot make your taxes go down. Unfortunately, you can accidentally make them go up - if you use corporations, as opposed to LLCs.

The IRS recognizes two kinds of corporations. One is an S corporation and another is a C corporation. Both of them are poor choices for landlords, the S corporation at least being acceptable. Not recommended, but still an acceptable entity for landlords.

The C Corporation, however, is totally, absolutely inappropriate for holding rental properties. In fact, one of my attorney friends said that he would consider it malpractice recommending a C corporation for a landlord.

So when we are choosing business entities, again, for landlords, I say rely on your attorney's recommendation for legal protection, as long as you are not creating a corporation. In particular, under all circumstances, avoid a C corporation.

Now, we are moving on to the other type of real estate business – flipping, wholesaling, realtors, contractors, or any other type of real estate entrepreneurs, other than landlords.

They have a very different set of entity recommendations, because their tax considerations become as important as legal protection and, sometimes, even more important.

I'm saying that because if you are a landlord and you own properties, exposure to legal liability can cost you losing your properties. But if you are, say, a wholesaler, you don't risk losing a property. So while your legal liabilities can still be significant, they may not be as significant as for people who hold properties.

However, tax considerations for flippers and wholesalers are far more important, and recommendations are different.

I now talk about corporations again. I said that corporations were inappropriate *for landlords*. On the flipping and wholesaling side, S corporations and C corporations are the two vehicles that can, under some circumstances, reduce your tax liability. And I stress, of course, under the right circumstances.

Often when discussing the terms of a real estate investor, a landlord is thought of as someone who is investing in real estate, while someone that's flipping houses or wholesaling, it's more like that's their job. Their active income would be the distinction. Is that how it's seen by the IRS?

Michael Plaks: Yes. Well, you mentioned the word investor, which is interpreted differently in so many contexts. Maybe it's worth spending a few minutes to clarify the word *investor*.

In our real estate investor community, we call an investor pretty much anybody who is involved with real estate.

But actually, the correct phrase should be a real estate business person or a real estate entrepreneur. We tend to use it interchangeably with investor.

Technically speaking, you cannot call a wholesaler investor at all, because outside of real estate, an investor means someone who puts his money into something for future profit.

Well, a wholesaler doesn't put his money into anything. There is no money at risk. Wholesalers work almost as realtors, essentially as matchmakers. So a wholesaler, in that respect, should not be called an investor.

From a tax law point of view, an investor is somebody who *owns* property at some point, and a wholesaler doesn't. A landlord owns properties, and a flipper owns properties during the construction period. Those two groups could be called investors for tax purposes. And they generate two different types of income: *active* or *earned* income (Schedule C) for flippers and *passive* income (Schedule E) for landlords.

If you drill even deeper, then we should distinguish between three types of income. Not two, but actually three types of income. The third is pure investment income (Schedule D).

It wouldn't really be a full-time, dedicated businessperson. It would be somebody who just on the side, casually owns a piece of real estate, holding it and then selling it at some point.

An example is somebody who inherited a piece of property from her family. She holds the land for a while and then ends up selling it. Is she truly a real estate investor in its usual sense? No, she is not spending her time finding deals and doing construction and management and so on. It is just some property that she happens to own, and she is not making a living from it. The IRS expects her property to go on the Schedule D of her tax return and be treated strictly as a capital gain type of transaction.

But this scenario is not common in the context that we are dealing with. These are not people who are actively involved in real estate - like landlords and flippers. For those two categories, the IRS uses the terms *passive* and *active* (or *earned*).

This choice of words is somewhat ironic, because if you look at a landlord, and the IRS calls that *passive* income, the word passive kind of implies that no work is being done. Well, that's how the tax laws actually treat landlords and their business. As if the only thing that the landlord is doing is sitting back and collecting rent checks and getting wealthier by the month.

Obviously, this rosy picture does not represent the reality of our business. But that's the tax law angle on the landlord's business, and it's referred to as passive income. There is one set of rules for passive income and for landlords.

Reselling income, on the other hand, is considered to be active income, or earned income, by the IRS. Another term often used is self-employment income. These terms apply to wholesaling and flipping businesses.

Even though these are just two terms, active and passive, there is actually a very big difference in taxation, right?

Michael Plaks: In taxation, yes, absolutely.

Go into a little bit about what the difference is because that's something very important that investors don't realize, and it's a dramatic difference.

Michael Plaks: Yes, the difference is very dramatic. The easiest way to show it is with an example.

Let's take a rental property, and this rental property is rented for $1,000 a month. So we have $12,000 rent collected from the house during the year.

Then we have expenses that we pay out on that property starting, of course, with the monthly mortgage payments. Let's assume that there is no escrow, for simplicity. Once a year we pay property taxes and insurance premiums.

We also pay for repairs, maintenance, and other operational costs. Let's add them up, and maybe we spend $10,000 on that property in various expenses: mortgage payments, insurance, taxes, maintenance, repairs, etc.

What do we have? There is $12,000 rent income and $10,000 of various expenses. In investor terms, we have a $2,000 annual cash flow. When we evaluate properties from an investor point of view, deciding if it's a good deal or not, the $2,000 cash flow figure is what we look at.

But when we prepare a tax return, we need to know how much *taxable income* we generated. To most investors' frustration, the answer is nothing even close to that $2,000 cash flow.

That's the biggest problem and confusion when a new investor starts learning about IRS taxes. The landlord investor thinks that since he spent $10,000, he must have $10,000 of tax deductions. But for the IRS calculations, the $10,000 figure means nothing.

First, you cannot count your mortgage payment as an expense. You can only count the *interest* portion of mortgage payments.

Second, what we normally call repairs, the IRS may or may not consider as repairs. Only if it qualifies as repairs under the IRS definition, only then we can deduct them.

For example, if we bought a $700 refrigerator for the property, for an investor, that's an expense. For the IRS, it's considered buying an *asset* for the rental property, and it cannot be deducted in full in the year of purchase. This $700 deduction must be spread over 5 years, using a very strange formula.

Another example, if we change a roof on a house, for an investor, that's an expense. For the IRS, it's a *capital improvement* to the property, and only a small portion of the total cost of the new roof, less than 5%, can be deducted right away. The rest of it will be deducted over many years in the future.

I mentioned two variations in calculating taxable income: mortgage interest and repairs. The third one is a tax deduction for something called *depreciation*, which is almost a phantom deduction, because nobody ever writes a check for depreciation.

Depreciation is a convoluted accounting gimmick that essentially allows you to gradually write off the cost of the property itself.

So, we discussed three distinctions. Instead of deducting the full mortgage payment, you only deduct the interest. Then you may have to treat some repairs as something other than repairs. And, finally, you add depreciation deduction.

As a result, even though in our example $2,000 was the cash flow, for tax calculations, on paper, it might show $12,000 of income and a total of, say, $13,000 in expenses including depreciation - showing that the property is *losing* $1,000 for tax purposes.

So what happens in this situation, that ideal situation for a landlord?

He does have actual cash flow coming into his pockets month in and month out. But at the end of the year, as far as the IRS is concerned, the investor is losing money. Which means not only is he not paying extra taxes on his rental income, but, in fact, he *reduces* his overall taxes. And that result is mostly due to the depreciation that we discussed.

I'd like to point out that, in our examples, the properties had mortgages. Generally, if you have a single-family rental property with a mortgage, in the tax calculations, it would show a loss most of the time.

Without a mortgage, rental properties are likely to show some positive taxable income, even after deducting depreciation. So let's say that the tax calculations do show that there is a $2,000 taxable income from that rental property, after all deductions and depreciation. This income (which is called *net* rental income) will be taxed at the rate that is your current tax bracket, whatever it is - 10%, 15%, 25% or higher.

Let's say it is 25%, in a very typical situation. The good news is that the investor does not owe any additional taxation for Social Security or Medicare. 25% income tax on the net income, after all expenses, and this is it.

That's how the IRS taxes work on the landlord side.

In sharp contrast to that, on the other side of the business, flipping and wholesaling, the taxes are much higher. Let me take wholesaling as an example. The wholesaler made a $2,000 assignment fee, after marketing costs and other expenses.

The wholesaler's $2,000 will be taxed not only at his regular bracket rate, such as 25%, but on top of that, the wholesaler will have to deal with what is known as *self-employment tax*, which is a combination of two taxes: Social Security tax and Medicare tax. Self-employment tax adds another 15% to the wholesaler's tax burden..

As we discussed a minute before, on the landlord side, the $2,000 income is taxed at 25%, and that's a $500 tax.

Compare this with the wholesaler. His $2,000 income is taxed at 25% *plus* 15% self-employment tax - a total of 40%, and that becomes an $800 tax.

So one guy made $2,000 and the other guy made $2,000. One pays $500 and the other pays $800 in tax. It's a huge difference. And with 10 properties, it will be the difference between $5,000 tax and $8,000 tax.

This is one example why the distinction between the two types of real estate businesses is absolutely critical for bookkeeping purposes and for taxation.

Even though people say, "I'm a real estate investor," depending on the activities that you do and how you position yourself and set up your business, you could be either seen by the IRS as making money or losing money.

You could make $20,000 and your actual expenses out of pocket may have been $15,000, but the IRS would see you as losing money.

Or, if you do it the other way, you could make $20,000 and actually spend $25,000 on expenses, but the IRS could see you as making money. Is that right?

Michael Plaks: Unfortunately, it is true, and it can be even worse.

I will give you an example. Say you bought a rental property for $100,000 and put $20,000 in repairs, so you invested $120,000 in that property. Now, after holding it for a few years, the property grew in value, which is called appreciation.

You are selling it for $150,000. So you made a $30,000 profit between your investment of $120,000 and selling it for $150,000. Of course, I'm oversimplifying by not considering closing costs and depreciation recapture, and all the other factors. I'm just trying to simplify the example to the bare bones.

So you made $30,000 from appreciation of this rental. That $30,000 will be taxed as long-term capital gains, which is 15% rate tax. 15% of $30,000 is $4,500 in taxes. It is a reasonable tax on the profit that you really made. Most people when looking at that will say, "Well, that's not too bad. I actually did make $30,000 on the property. I only paid a reasonable $4,500 to the government." Of course, none of us wants to pay even a dollar to the government, but that is taxation that you can consider more or less fair.

As a side note, this $4,500 capital gain tax can be postponed using an advanced strategy known as a *1031 exchange*. It would not be worth it in my example. The numbers are too small. But on a bigger capital gain, you may want to consider a 1031 exchange. It could spare you from paying $4,500 at the time of sale.

Now, let's look at a completely different business model, flipping, but we will use the same numbers. We take the same exact deal, only now as a flip, not as a rental. We buy a $100,000 house and put $20,000 into repairs, so we have $120,000 invested in the house.

We sell it two months later at a $150,000 sale price. We made a $30,000 profit on this flip. Again, for simplicity I'm ignoring all complications like closing costs, financing costs, holding costs, and all the other costs.

To make the example more interesting, let's owner-finance that property, which is common nowadays. So you owner finance that property, and you collect a $5,000 down payment. You receive no other money in the year of sale, only the down payment. The rest will be paid to you later.

The IRS will say, "Wait a second." You had a property that you sold for a $30,000 profit. That was a flip and not a rental, so the 15% long-term capital gain rate does not apply. We must use the current tax bracket rate, possibly 25%. On top of that, we have to add the self-employment tax, and we are now looking at a 40% combined tax. Actually, 40% may be a little bit of an exaggeration, because it very rarely goes that high. But it's totally realistic to have a 33% combined rate for these two taxes. So let's use the 33% combined tax rate.

And here comes the deal killer. Because it is a flip, the IRS will demand that you pay tax on the *full amount* of profit - the entire $30,000 - up front, despite the fact that you only received $5,000 as a down payment. In other words, the IRS collects taxes on the money that you have not yet received! It is very unfair, but it is the law.

How bad it is? Pretty bad. 33% tax rate, or 1/3 of the $30,000 profit, is $10,000. You owe a $10,000 tax to the IRS. Ouch!

Think about it: you have the $5,000 down payment that you received and a $10,000 IRS bill on the money that you have not yet received. Not only your entire down payment goes to the IRS, but you have to add another $5,000 out of your pocket!

I think with this example you can clearly see that taxation of a sold property can be drastically different between the two types of real estate businesses.

In the case of a rental property, you have a reasonably small amount of taxes, at the 15% rate that can be deferred with a 1031 exchange.

In the case of an owner-financed flip, you have an absolutely brutal 30-40% taxation that, by the way, you cannot defer because 1031 exchanges are not available for flips. Only for rentals..

See why it's so important to have proper tax classification and consider exit strategies and their tax implications before you finalize the deal.

That's why having a tax professional on your team is not an expense, but actually where your money is made.

With the right advice and the right strategies, from what you just demonstrated, it makes a big difference. That's the difference between paying a small piece of what you earned to the government for taxes and owing the government more than you actually put in your pocket.

Many investors think that there are tax loopholes. "I can save on taxes by taking advantage of this hidden secret - or I heard about this way that you can get around that tax."

You don't deal in loopholes, do you? You deal in optimizing what the government and the IRS put out there as the options, although they don't make them very clear, right?

So what you do best is take what is legally available, and you're able to optimize that for your clients?

Michael Plaks: You brought up a point that is very important to me, and that I often discuss with my first-time clients.

When you pointed out that the cost of using professional services is not really a cost but a money-saving investment, that doesn't just apply to me. It is true about any professional you include on your team: a Realtor, a staging expert, an attorney, an accountant, and, of course, contractors.

One of my colleagues, John Hyre, who is a real estate attorney, an accountant, and an investor himself, said it best. He said, "When I talk to my clients who ask about the cost of my service, I tell them that I cost less. Then they look at my rates and see that my hourly rate is $250! And I clarify - I didn't say I was cheap. I said I *cost less*."

Which means that if you are not using professional service, you will end up paying more in the end. It is very true.

Yes, you can sell a house without a Realtor. But unless you are a skilled salesperson and a legal expert yourself, you rarely come out ahead. You will have to pay a commission to your Realtor, but in the end, you will sell it higher, faster, and you will end up saving money and avoid very costly mistakes.

It's the same with my services. Yes, you are going to have to pay for my service. I always tell people, "You might be able to pay $200 less for tax preparation elsewhere. But, if they do it wrong, it can easily cost you $2,000 in unnecessary taxes paid to the IRS. Which is more important to you - $200 or $2,000?"

We're comparing the wrong types of numbers. Instead of looking at what it costs to hire a professional, you need to look at what it may cost to *not* hire one. Or hire a wrong one.

On my website, I quote Red Adair, the famous oil well firefighter. He said: "If you think it's expensive to hire a professional to do the job, wait until you hire an amateur."

Now, let's talk about the loopholes that you mentioned. It depends on the definition. They say that there're two kinds of misunderstanding. Either we call the same thing two different names, or we call two different things the same name.

So when we say loopholes, there are different kinds of loopholes, and let's agree which kind we're discussing.

Some loopholes are completely legitimate exceptions to the rules. They are called loopholes not because they break the rules, but because they are not very well known.

For example, we briefly talked about 1031 exchanges. You can call it a loophole, because it is a little-known strategy that allows you to avoid paying capital gains tax at the time of sale. It does provide a major relief from taxes, but it is perfectly legal. The IRS will not have any objection to using that technique.

Another example of a perfectly legal loophole is a technique called 'Asset Segregation' or 'Cost Segregation', which are just two different terms for the same technique. It allows you to dramatically increase your depreciation deduction. Sometimes, you can triple your depreciation, as I show on examples when I teach my taxation classes.

While asset segregation is a completely legal loophole, it is in a different group, because the IRS does not like this technique and frequently audits returns with unusually high depreciation. I do encourage clients under the right circumstances to use it, but I always warn them about an increased risk of an IRS audit.

In other words, we have some legal loopholes that the IRS readily accepts, and other, also legal, loopholes that the IRS does not like and often audits.

And then there are a whole lot of other things that people refer to as loopholes, but those go against the rules and are not legal.

I've heard people say, "We can look at that transaction and call it something else. It's not what really happened, but if we call it something else and put it in a different category, then it would be taxed much better."

Here is an example of a so-called loophole that I've actually heard promoted at a real estate webinar. Let's take that same deal that I was talking about, the wholesale deal or the flip deal, and report it under another entity tax return. Let's put it inside an S corporation or a partnership.

See, normally, the amount of tax should not change when you use entities. A partnership and an S corporation are two entities that are called 'flow-through entities,' meaning that they do not pay their own taxes. The result of their activity transfers to the owner's personal tax returns, and the owner pays taxes on their personal income and on their business income, combined.

Basically, you report your business under a partnership or an S corporation and calculate business profit or loss. Then you transfer this profit or loss to your personal return through a form known as a K-1. That form tells how much money you made or lost in your partnership or S Corporation.

Now, what those "creative" people do during that transition is they change the classification of the income. So if their partnership or an S corporation sold a flip, they report it on K-1 as passive income, which supposedly "avoids" the 15% self-employment tax.

Is it a loophole? Depends on how you look at it. If you ask what are the chances that the IRS will notice? - the answer is that they probably won't. Is it a loophole, then? Did it save you money? You can say yes. But, if challenged by the IRS, it won't hold any water, because you cannot legally change the classification of income simply by checking a different box on a form.

Those types of loopholes pretend to save you money, but they do so by breaking the rules and breaking the law. I cannot endorse it, and I will never use it with my clients.

Finally, there is one other type of what we can call loopholes. It is the famous "grey area" which unfortunately is huge. Grey area, when it comes to taxes, is both attractive and frustrating for investors.

On one hand, you have tax-saving ideas that are perfectly legal, like 1031 exchanges, asset segregation, or self-directed IRAs. On the other hand, you have things like reclassifying the type of income on K-1 that is clearly not okay and not legal.

And then you have this gigantic zone in between, which you can look at in multiple ways, and it has to do with the uncertainty of our business.

For example, you bought a property, fixed it, rented for a couple of months, and then sold to the tenant. Was it a flip, or was it a rental? Your answer determines how much tax you owe on this deal, so it is really important. Yet, there is no black-and-white answer in this situation.

In many situations like that, the answers are up in the air and subject to debate and interpretation. If you like clarity and certainty, you will hate these situations. If you enjoy challenge and creativity, you may actually welcome the fact that the tax laws are so unclear and confusing.

Unfortunately, like I said, there is no simple way to resolve many tax situations. This is where the value of an experienced accountant specializing in real estate can be enormous.

We can look at your specific transaction, at your specific deal, and advise you and tell you if there is room for creative interpretation. We can tell you the consequences and how much you can save. We'll also describe to you the risks that come with more aggressive positions.

Then, you can make your own informed decision, which balances your tax savings and your risk exposure.

The consequences of not using someone who is a professional and an expert are obvious.

But there are people who don't do that, even though they know that it's the right thing to do and that it's going to be in their best interest. They feel that they've screwed up so badly already. They are a mess, and they are ashamed and embarrassed to go seek someone because of all the mess they already made out of their business.

Real estate investors oftentimes are not the best at bookkeeping or understanding this kind of stuff.

So what would you say to someone that might have a shoebox of receipts? They might have scribbles in a book of what their expenses have been. They know what they need to do, but they might be worried or ashamed to come to someone like you because of that situation.

I'm assuming that you probably don't make judgments. You try to work with what's there and get them on track, right?

Michael Plaks: No, I do not judge my clients who are behind, who lost money, who made huge mistakes, who are disorganized or who are in any other kind of trouble. I have seen it all, and I understand that life happens.

Besides, I had my share of my personal troubles and mistakes, too. Nobody is perfect.

I can relate when someone procrastinates addressing very important issues in his life, be it health or accounting, which by the way is also health - financial health.

Mental health, too. A lot of people don't realize it.

Michael Plaks: Certainly. I have helped many clients who were in severe distress over their tax problems. I keep a box of tissues on my desk for a reason. Some visitors need it.

You know, it's the best feeling in the world to watch someone's burden lifted from her shoulders, after we took care of her issues. I love this part of my job.

People who are behind on taxes and bookkeeping, they are motivated to come to me by two different sets of circumstances.

One is when they come voluntarily. They basically reach a point where they decide they've waited long enough. It's time for them to clean things up and face the music.

The second one is, unfortunately, when they are forced to come. The IRS is already knocking on their door or, worse, trying to intercept their paychecks or bank accounts. I have a large number of clients who come with those drastic situations.

Either way, when you have to catch up with many years of unfiled taxes, and I do have clients that have not filed taxes for ten years and more, there are a couple of things that I want people in such situations to keep in mind. Good and bad. I'll start with the bad.

The bad part is: if you did not file a tax return, there is no expiration for your liability. There is no statute of limitations on that, and that's a common misunderstanding. People believe that after a certain number of years, the IRS cannot ask you for your tax return. Wrong. If a tax return has never been filed, you are always technically liable for that return.

Nothing stops the IRS from pursuing you for your 2005 tax return, which is ten years back, if you never filed it, as long as you owe money for that year. So, if in that year, you had a profitable business and owed money, well, you're on the hook for that forever, until you file a return. That's the bad part.

The good part, however, is that in order to prepare a tax return, you do not actually need to have a complete set of receipts and documents, which a lot of people do not understand.

True, in order to file a tax return, you have to have an accurate set of *numbers*. What happens if you don't have an accurate set of numbers, for whatever reason? Then your next best thing is to have a good reasonable estimate of those numbers. Creating a tax return based on reasonable estimates is legal. And I stress - reasonable. It cannot be total fiction.

Now, the question that follows is: will the IRS accept such tax return? Accept - yes. Will the IRS give you trouble later? Well, the IRS can audit any return during the three years after it is filed. Whether you are filing a current tax return for the last year or finally filing an old return that is ten years late - the IRS has three years to audit it. Sometimes they do. Most of the time, they don't.

If the audit does happen, that is the only time when having receipts and other proof will be important. You will have to deal with it then, should you be unlucky to draw the IRS attention.

So what I encourage people to do, people who are behind multiple years, is to start by establishing certain estimates. We can prepare old tax returns based on those estimates and at least get the process going.

It's far better than sitting and doing nothing because, again, like I said, that liability never disappears on its own.

I am often asked for help when the old records are missing.

If you go to my website and look through the large number of free articles and blog posts that I published there for my clients and for everybody else who is not my client yet, one of the articles describes practical techniques to reconstruct your missing records and produce good estimates, so you can get the ball rolling on delinquent tax returns.

One of the greatest values that you provide is the fact that you give people the courage to take that step to get their business in order.

In addition to financial health, this really has a lot to do with people's mental health. It keeps people up at night. It gives people ulcers. It stresses them out.

You provide answers and insights, even on your website, into those things that people worry about when they're not sure exactly what they're worried about.

How can people find out more about Michael Plaks and how to get in contact with you and to see some of this great content that you have out there?

Michael Plaks: As far as mental health, I want to share a story that I think is kind of funny. Years ago, I used to mention on all my promotional pieces and my advertising that the benefit of working with me was peace of mind. It was prominently featured on my website.

Then, more than ten years ago, I received a very stern letter from the legal department of H&R Block, who claimed that 'peace of mind' was their trademark on which I was infringing. They threatened to unleash their legal army on me.

Well, me being me, I could not help writing back with a sarcastic response, and I will gladly share those back-n-forth letters for their entertainment value. In fact, I took it as a compliment that a huge national corporation, the giant H&R Block, considered my modest business a threat to their copyright. I must have made it.

But seriously, the truth remains that peace of mind is probably the greatest benefit that you can receive from working with our company, and we have heard this from our clients over and over again. You can read our online reviews.

Our clients tell us that they know, after doing things right, they don't have to be worried about overpaying unnecessary taxes on their hard-earned money, and they sleep well knowing that the IRS is not going to be after them. And if the IRS ever does decide to bother them, they will be in good shape.

As far as getting in touch with me, the best way to start is by visiting our website at www.MichaelPlaks.com.

The website is fairly easy to navigate. You can find a lot of free articles, a blog, list of upcoming classes and presentations, as well as recordings of past classes that are available for purchase.

Speaking of classes, I often do seminars and presentations. Most of them are conducted at the various realty investments clubs in the Houston area. By the way, we're starting online webinars in 2015.

Also on our website is a section titled 'Hire Michael Plaks' that explains how we approach our business, how we build relationships with our clients and what the next steps are. And, of course, you can call our office.

One thing we cannot accommodate is a walk-in, because we are very busy. So, if you want to visit us, please call us. We'll be happy to schedule an appointment.

Again, our website is the best starting place which I welcome everybody to visit. And, while there, make sure to subscribe to our newsletter, which is free.

Good luck in your business and your life!

About Michael Plaks

Michael Plaks is the go-to tax accountant for Houston real estate investors and is well known for his expert knowledge and his quirky personality. His business is rated as one of the top 3 tax services in Houston. Michael works exclusively with real estate investors, having prepared thousands of tax returns since 1996 and consulted hundreds of investors from all over the country.

He is a Federally licensed Enrolled Agent (EA) with extensive experience helping investors with IRS audits and other stressful matters. Michael is also an accomplished writer and an award-winning public speaker, frequently teaching classes and seminars on real estate bookkeeping and taxes.

Business Name: IRS Help – Michael Plaks, EA

Website: MichaelPlaks.com

Facebook: Facebook.com/MichaelPlaks.EA

LinkedIn: LinkedIn.com/in/MichaelPlaks

YouTube: YouTube.com/user/PlaksMichael/videos

REAL ESTATE BROKER

Shelly Walzel is a real estate broker who wears many hats when working with the real estate investor market in Houston, Texas. She often finds herself using the skills of a psychologist, sociologist and anthropologist to guide the investors she works with.

Her wide knowledge base from fifteen years as a real estate agent, and her personal experiences as an investor herself, has made her the expert that everyone wants to use. In this interview, Shelly discusses the obstacles that new and seasoned investors might run into and how she helps them overcome those obstacles. She also shares some of her strategies for making sure that her clients reach their personal investment goals.

'Real estate broker' is probably your technical or academic title, but you really do fall into the categories of psychologist, sociologist and anthropologist because you have to get inside the mind of your potential clients. Ultimately, your goal is to help them become successful real estate investors, not just help them find houses.

What does that successful investor looks like? What are they made up of, what is their mindset, and what level are they at to be able to work successfully with you and your team?

Shelly Walzel: I have seen all different types of investors coming into the real estate game at all different levels.

Just because you're inexperienced and don't know what you're doing doesn't mean you can't be as successful as that experienced investor, as long as you have the right team in place.

That's the whole idea here. Get your team together. Don't do it alone.

Make sure that you speak with each one of your team members: your contractor, your insurance agent, your broker, your lender, your significant other. Make sure that everybody is on the same page so you can move forward and reach that end goal that you have in mind.

A lot of people in a lot of entrepreneurial pursuits become a one-man game, but just about any successful entrepreneur investor relies on others to help them ultimately make that final choice. But it's very difficult to do it all on your own and have that much knowledge and expertise.

Shelly Walzel: That's right. As the broker, what I would say to that investor is, "You don't need to go and paint the house yourself. It's going to take you a week. Pay somebody to paint it so you can get the house back on the market." Or, "You don't need to take a tile class and lay that tile. That's why God made contractors."

If investors don't get in at the right time, or if they don't buy correctly, a lot of times the numbers aren't right. Then you find yourself backpedalling and doing the work yourself, which costs you more money and more time.

So, it is really important that your numbers are right. It's not an emotional game. It's a numbers business game going in, and it's important that you keep it that way.

I'll tell you another thing that I see a lot of people do. They think it's their house when they buy it. They are emotionally invested in the property. They'll buy this clunker of a house and have these grand beautiful ideas.

It's because they love real estate. They want to make this house look fantastic and beautiful. But, it doesn't necessarily get them more money at the closing table.

So they're putting in hardwood floors and they're painting with custom paints and upgrading all the fixtures to be top-notch fixtures. Really, it's not necessary and a lot of investors are overspending.

Yes, it's easy to let that spending get away from you. That's when you would need to take on the psychologist role to rein them in.

What different types of investors do you come across and what are their goals for investing in real estate?

Shelly Walzel: That's the first thing that I ask them, "What do you want out of it?" You have to know what you want out of it before you go into it.

I have some investors who want a monthly cash flow. They want rental property and they just want to live off of the monthly cash flow so they don't have to get "a real job."

I have other investors who want to pay off the house that they live in and they have a $200,000 balance. So they want $200,000.

There is a difference on how you would play this real estate game based on what your end game is. If you want monthly cash flow, you may be more inclined to have rental properties and make money that way. And that's just the tip of the iceberg.

If you're buying rental properties because you want cash flow, then you need to know how to make your numbers work so that after you pay taxes, insurance and HOA fees, cash flow is coming in. You have to buy the right property for that to happen.

If you are an investor that wants a chunk of money, flipping might be better for you. It might be easier for you to flip and gain $50,000 towards your house note if that is your end game.

So how you proceed is based on what you want out of it. But first you need to know what you want.

That puts a spotlight on the value of what you do. You see a lot of people saying, "The right way to do real estate is to buy and hold." Others say, "No, the right way to do real estate is quick flips for cash."

You don't make a judgment on what they want. There is no 'the right way.' It's the right way for this particular person's circumstances and the goals that they want.

Shelly Walzel: That's right. We have this debate all the time. Is it better to have your house paid off or is it better to have the interest deduction? One is not right or wrong. It's just different, with different risk levels and different perspectives.

Some people that think real estate is a risk, in the same way they think about black jack or slot machines – let's roll the dice and cross our fingers.

But because you are such a numbers person, it doesn't require a lot of guesswork or luck if you follow a formula, and there's a way to follow that formula that keeps people in what you call a 'safety zone' with their money, right?

Shelly Walzel: That's right.

For those who think they risk losing everything when investing, you say there are ways to invest and formulas you can use which help avoid some risk.

When you see a successful real estate investor, what is the formula and what are the principles that they're using that keep them in this game for the long term and makes them come out wealthy at the end of the day?

Shelly Walzel: Everyone has their own set of "I'm okay with this but I'm not okay with that."

I can tell you what I do when I buy a rental property or flip a house. If I don't see a profit on paper of more than $20,000, it's not worth it for me. The reason that it's not worth it to me is because there could be hidden costs I don't know about until after I've purchased the house, for example a termite infestation.

Or, I bought a house at auction and when the people left they tore up the house or took the appliances, so I need to buy new appliances.

You need to leave room for things you didn't think of or mistakes.

So for me, $20,000 is my limit. If it's less than $20,000, I'm out. There are tons of deals out there and a lot of properties to choose from. You don't have to go for every deal. You can take your time. You can go slowly and choose the ones that keep you in your comfort zone and in your safety zone.

The safety zone, obviously, is going to be at a different level for different people.

Shelly Walzel: Agreed.

On the other side of this, there are investors who get really gung ho and jump in without consulting you first. What do you say to these types of investors?

Shelly Walzel: Here's what I tell them. "In the end, I'm going to be selling that house for you. So we need to buy well enough so that if you have to put it on the market the very next day after you buy it, you're not going to lose any money."

I'm going to be responsible for selling it later, so I want the numbers to look good for every situation the investor might find themselves in.

That's important because a lot of investors may not consider every situation when making decisions. Having someone like you on the team helps them have the confidence they are making a good decision.

You also help them decide when this might not be the right house and it's probably best to walk away.

Shelly Walzel: That's right. You learn that quickly in this business. There's a learning curve that happens after the first investment when you feel that your numbers are a little too close to what you're comfortable spending. It's based on how many nights you stay awake at night. If you're not sleeping well, then we need to adjust your risk level.

Another thing that I want to put on the table is how the contract is written. I've never lost money in real estate. Not on any transaction and I've done many in my fifteen years of selling real estate.

The reason why is because you can write a contract to protect you up until the very last day - up until closing day. So, you're not losing earnest money and you're not losing any of your options. We do this to protect all of your dollars every step of the way until you know this is going to be the deal that you want.

A lot of people don't understand contracts and assume that this is the way it is and it's the standard way to do it.

Which situation do people seem to be more disappointed about, or more on edge about - when they're trying to make a decision to buy a property, or when you've had to tell them that it's probably better to walk away from a deal that they've gotten invested in emotionally and had plans to do, but something pops up?

Which one of those is harder to do?

Shelly Walzel: Great question. It depends on the person and their personal situation. Do I really want to have five flips by the end of the year? Do I want to make my hundred thousand dollars just on my flipping?

If that's the case, you're more apt to jump in and get the job done. But, it depends on the personality type. I know some investors who are terrified of the unknown.

But here's the thing. I can write the contract showing them getting a loan and not paying with cash. I can write it so that if something happens and they can't get that loan, they get their earnest money back and haven't lost anything.

So, the fear of jumping in isn't as scary as long as the contract is written correctly and you know your numbers. That's part of the process – making sure everything is in place so you can jump in with confidence.

As a real estate broker, you're probably going to be the person that an investor's going to rely on the most to help navigate the contract, right?

Shelly Walzel: Yes.

Especially in Texas, because the Texas real estate contract is not that simple. There are a lot of lines to it.

Some people say, "Here, just sign this. It's a standard contract." Is there really such a thing as a standard contract? How much latitude do people have to adjust that contract and really make it fit the circumstances?

Shelly Walzel: You absolutely can adjust the contract and this is why you need a real estate agent because you want to make sure you protect yourself as much as possible.

There is a Texas Real Estate Commission (TREC) standard contract, but there are a lot of blanks in that contract. You need somebody that knows what you're trying to get out of it so they know how to write that contract to benefit that investor.

Even though the TREC contract is a standard contract, there are a lot of blanks in it. The way those blanks are filled out can really be advantageous to either party, depending on how they're filled out, right?

Shelly Walzel: That's right.

So when people say it's just a standard contract, what would you tell an investor about how to respond if somebody handed them something and said, "Here, it's just a standard contract?"

Shelly Walzel: Well, I would want to see that contract with the client so I can help them understand the contract says and answer any questions they may have.

If they told me it was standard, I'd say, "I understand its standard, but what about this? We want more days here and less days there." We want to make sure it's dated for when we want – perhaps closing in 10 days instead of 30 days because we want to get this on the market within a certain time frame. Or, we want to close in 45 days because we need more time to get funding.

Depending on the situation for that investor, we have to write that contract to fit that investor's needs and to benefit the investor not the seller.

Like it or not, the fact is a lot of people have gotten into investing over the last decade because of what they've seen on reality shows

Based on your real world experience, what do you see new investors being completely uneducated about based on what they see on reality shows, versus what real successful investors encounter on a day-to-day basis?

Shelly Walzel: Well, you watch a 30-minute show and during this 30 minutes, they buy the home at a great price, fix it up, and sell it at double the price. You don't get to see the sleepless nights and you don't get to see them talking to the contractors, or two or three different contractors, and finding out which one can give you the best price. There are a lot of steps in there that you don't get to see.

You don't see them writing the contract at the very beginning to protect the buyer so they can close and close well. Or, making sure that the numbers are right. There are a lot of steps in there that you miss, both good and bad. But it is definitely a Hollywood version on TV. It's the rose-colored glasses type of view.

It's fascinating how they sell the home for double its worth on these shows.

Some people think, "You've got to put a lot of money into a home and add top of the line upgrades on your home to get the highest price."

Often people feel their home is worth so much more because of the upgrades they have added. But in Texas, Mr. Appraiser may not feel the same way, regardless of what someone's willing to pay for it.

Shelly Walzel: Just because somebody puts their house on the market for $400,000 where houses are selling from $200,000 to $300,000, doesn't mean they're going to get that price.

This is another reason why you need a realtor when you enter the market. When you buy a home, you need your realtor to tell you not to buy it for $400,000 if it's only worth between $200,000 and $300,000. We are still going to have to go in and fix it up. And then, we're going to have to sell it.

Then, if we don't have a cash buyer, it will have to be appraised by an appraiser and it won't appraise for your asking price. Which means your buyer will not get funding and you're going to be back to square one.

In the end, know your numbers. A realtor shows them the numbers. A realtor can tell them where to price their home to get the highest price.

So even if a buyer came and offered you $400,000, unless they're paying cash, that ultimate decision isn't up to them whether the house is going to be sold for that amount?

Shelly Walzel: That's right. Now, having said that, let's just say we have an investor buyer who's sitting on $300,000 in cash. They buy this house and pay cash for it and they want to seller finance it when they sell it.

I know this is a whole different scenario than we were talking about, but let's just say that investor puts it on the market for $400,000, finds a buyer and seller finances it with $100,000 up front. There is no outside lender involved so no appraisal is necessary. Now he has cash flow coming in for the next three to five years, when there's a balloon payment due and he will get the rest of his cash back. He not only made $100,000. But also is making interest on the $300,000 loan to the buyer.

There are so many different ways to do this. I know I'm throwing a lot on the table at one time, but I'm doing it so you can see that every investor has a different plan.

Yes, and that's another reason an investor would want to work with an experienced realtor that can present alternatives when selling properties.

It is also important to note that when a real estate agent or broker shows you those numbers, they are basing those numbers off of properties that have been sold in the same area. Some beginners that want *to dabble in investing will go to MLS and HAR and think "I can buy this house for this amount, and homes are selling for $300,000 in this neighborhood."*

Is this when you would tell a client, "Wait a minute. You're basing that off of what you're seeing on the public HAR? HAR shows what houses are NOT selling for."

Shelly Walzel: Exactly. You need to look at the Sold comps, not the Active comps.

So when investors look at HAR and the MLS, and they see homes for $200,000 or $300,000, the reality is they're seeing what homes aren't selling for.

How can investors see what homes are really selling for and what the benefit is of working with a brokered agent to get that information?

Shelly Walzel: Okay. When we do comps as agents, we talk about wants and facts. Active homes on the market are wants. It's not a fact.

It's great information to have, but when you're doing the numbers, it's the sold numbers you want. Those are the facts. That's what really happened in the market and that's where everybody settled on a price. That is what you need know.

So you're right about that. Actives are dreams. They're the people with a house on the market, waiting to see if it works. The Solds are the facts.

A good real estate agent or broker is almost like an interpreter. They go behind the scenes and look at the Solds. Typically, those comps are restricted to the licensed agents.

When you see those comps, sometimes you actually have unfolded a story on that house that no one would ever have seen from the outside. Also someone that doesn't have an eye or experience in real estate may not recognize the story that you see.

There are elements in there that show how the price has been adjusted over time or the last time that house was sold, and maybe other important information that could be relevant to a decision on that house.

What are some of the things you see in those comps that help you interpret that story?

Shelly Walzel: When you look at your comps, you want to look at several different things. Here's what I look for.

I want to see if it has granite counters or other upgrades. Does it have a swimming pool? What size lot is it on? What amenities does the neighborhood have? All that will count for that particular house and why it sold for the price that it sold for.

Something else that is really important to know is your real estate agent, a lot of times, has inside information. Perhaps we know that house has been on the market before. Last year, they tried to put it on the market at a different price than it is listed for this time. That's really good information to know and it helps when we go to bid on the home. When we place an offer, all of that information is very helpful in making sure that we get our client the best price.

Maybe we know the "bus stop talk". What I call "bus stop talk" is where all the mothers get together when the kids get on the bus in the morning and stand around and talk about so-and-so's being transferred and they have to sell the house within 90 days. That's great information.

Yes. A lot of people may not know how to interpret the data they see back there that could be key for a decision process.

Investors need to understand exactly what could be revealed when seeing the comps, as opposed to what most people think they're seeing when they look at HAR from the public side. The public HAR is just a small layer of the story.

Shelly Walzel: That's true. As real estate agents, we talk to each other. Let's say I'm representing my investor buyer and they're interested in a house. I may go to the agent who's listing that property and say, "Hey, do you have other offers? What can you tell me? What's it going to take to get this house?"

Some agents are more forthcoming with information than others but, it doesn't hurt to try and get as much information about that particular house that your client wants to buy so you can position your contract or your offer in the perfect way.

Maybe that seller is having a house built and they really need to be there for another 60 days. If that's the house that you want, perhaps you can hold off the closing for 60 days. It'll make you look like the better buyer in a multiple offer situation.

They will choose you over somebody else because they will have the convenience of staying in their home for another month.

That's very important. It comes back to the psychology and the sociology and understanding that commitment and currency doesn't always come in front of a dollar sign. You can position your offer to be the one to be chosen, even if it may not be the highest monetarily.

Shelly Walzel: That's right. One thing that I've learned in this business is that somebody might say, "If I'm the seller, I would never pay closing costs for a buyer." Okay, fine. So closing costs is a no-no. I get it.

If you're going to ask for $6,000 in closing costs, maybe you don't call it closing costs. Maybe we call it a repair allowance. Or maybe we take it off the price of the home. There are a lot of different ways to get $6,000.

Yes. It's all about framing that offer.

One of the reasons a real estate broker or agent plays a cornerstone in an investor's team is the fact that you have seen so many different situations and so many different types of transactions. As a result, you not only can help and advise people on choosing the home, but you sometimes see red flags come up with the lender that they might be working with. Or, you see red flags come up with the title company where this transaction might be occurring.

You have a lot of insight into the rest of the transaction that a lot of other service providers don't have. For example, title companies are mystery to a lot of people.

What exactly happens at the title company? What can go right or wrong? Are they helping the buyer or are they helping the seller? What do I need to watch out for? What does the title company do?

Shelly Walzel: The purpose of the title company is to make sure that the title of the home is clear when the buyer closes. They make sure that there are no liens on the property when you close. They produce the title policy.

So they insure the transfer of the property is true and complete. They make sure that you own it and nobody else can stake any kind of claim on that property. Once you close on it, it's your property.

And as they're doing their title searches, the title company needs to make sure that the right people sign off on it.

This is a more complicated example, but let's say the seller was married then divorced and then remarried again. We need to know, through that chain of ownership, who signs off on it so there are no issues later. That's what a title company does. They make sure that once you close nobody else can come back and say they own part of that home. They make sure the past is all corrected so you won't have problems in the future.

They provide insurance saying that if someone does come back, it's on them, to a certain extent, right?

Shelly Walzel: Right. When they clear the title, they supply that owner's title policy and that's the insurance policy. So, if anybody ever comes back and says, "I'm the long lost son and my dad passed away. I get 25% of this house, therefore, I own 25% of your house." The title policy will protect the new owner.

I see some investors who want to bypass the title companies. When somebody wants to do that, it's time to step away. Somebody's going to loose. You must go through the right chain of ownership on this and that title policy is important for that purpose.

Most people can't fathom that this is possible. There have been a ton of "get rich" courses on real estate that teach people how to do what they call the 'kitchen table closing.'

The fact is tracing ownership of the house can be as simple as signing the deed. A lot of people think there has to be something else going on, but that's what the title company does. They make sure all the t's are crossed and i's are dotted when the deed is signed over.

But it's not something that's required in Texas.

Shelly Walzel: They also do handshake closings in Texas where people shake hands and they say, "It's yours." It's not a good idea.

But it is possible. That's frightening.

I'm sure you've helped quite a few investors sell their houses after you helped them acquire it and they've done their work. What are some of the things that you do to help them avoid surprises before they go and sell? You said a lot of investors get emotional about this. Do you see a lot of them that try to mimic the reality shows and just go way overboard on pricing this house?

Shelly Walzel: Yes, I do. In my opinion, a house that is priced right, especially in this market, can bring in more money than a house that's overpriced.

If a house is overpriced, it may sit on the market for a month. Nobody's buying it. A lot of people are looking at it, but it's overpriced and buyers don't want to pay that price.

Then before long, it's passed x amount of days where people are now thinking, "What's wrong with the house?" By the time you're ready to say, "Okay, I've overpriced it," and you start lowering the price, then people are thinking, "First they've overpriced it. And now they're dropping the price like crazy." Before you know it, you've lost.

If you had just priced it right in the first place, you would have come out ahead, and done it quicker.

You're able to tell them maybe they shouldn't do that painting or flooring. People think, "I'll add a bathroom here because it'll raise the value."

When you talk about getting a better price, is it's not necessarily about getting a better price. It's about getting a better profit out of a house, right?

Shelly Walzel: Absolutely. If you spend $10,000 to put that bathroom in and then you have to raise your price $10,000, what have you done? You've just spent a lot of time and there's no gain.

That's one of the good things about you because you are a numbers person. You help people by finding out if their goal is to have the prettiest house on the market, or if their goal is to make a profit as quickly as possible.

Shelly Walzel: Right. There are investors out there who just really want to be known for having the prettiest homes by the time they're done. And that's okay.

But there are also investors who are in it for the money, and most of them are. And it's because of the huge, very lucrative business that this is. They don't want to lose money. So different people want different things out of it.

So, you're not there to judge. You're there to help them get the outcome that they want to achieve.

Shelly Walzel: Right. In my perfect scenario, I would like to see if an investor buys a home that doesn't sell for what they wanted, then they could also put it on the market to rent.

The numbers are different if you want to rent it or sell it. You look at it from a different perspective.

So, in my perfect scenario, the perfect house to purchase would have a couple of different exit strategies. If one didn't work exactly the way you wanted it, then maybe, you seller finance it. Or maybe you rent it. Or maybe you do something else.

I'd like to see a couple of different ways to exit that property and not just one, if possible.

Always have contingencies by making sure you have a couple of different exit plans.

New investors may see using an agent, or using a broker, as an additional cost. Smart investors have the mindset that using the right agent or broker makes them money.

How do people change that scarcity mindset of not using a broker or an agent because it's going to cost them money, into the mindset of if they use the right broker or agent, it's going to make them money?

Shelly Walzel: There are two sides to that. As far as buying a house, it's the seller that pays the commission, not the buyer. It's the seller's listing broker that pays the other agent the commission that they collect from the seller.

So, the seller pays that listing broker, let's say 6%. Of course, all of this is negotiable, but let's say 6% commission. That listing agent will collect 6%.

If that buyer comes along and buys the house without an agent, that listing broker will still be collecting that 6%. Now, the buyer has nobody to represent him.

So the money is going to be collected one way or the other on that side of it.

On the flip side of that, some people think, "I'll stick a sign in the yard or I'll do a For Sale By Owner to make more money." Why is it that smart investors understand that using an agent to sell their house is going to make them money, either price-wise or time-wise?

Shelly Walzel: That's right. Why does a seller need an agent?

A seller needs an agent, first of all, to read and write contracts that will benefit them. In addition, they need to make sure that you're comp'd out correctly in the neighborhood so you do get the most for your money.

Maybe a seller's agent will come in and tell the seller, "You need to take half the things out of this room so buyers can see how big the room is." Or, they can show them how to stage their home to make it look the way a potential buyer will want to see it. The seller's agent will suggest they take a lot of the personal pictures out of the home or depersonalize the home.

There are a lot of different areas that an agent can come in and help you with, and contracts is just one of those.

By the way, the lender will not speak with the seller. So, if a buyer brings an offer to the table and you accept it and they have their lender, that lender will only speak with the buyer's agent. That seller can't go to that lender, because it's a privacy issue.

So now, you're completely out of the loop. You're in the defensive position. Everybody's doing things around you and you have no control over anything. You're just hoping it all goes well.

I would want somebody representing me that can take control of the situation and make sure the contract benefits me. Make sure my timeframe's in there. Make sure that potential buyer is a qualified buyer, especially if they are walking through your home.

Yes, that's an important part. There are people that can waste a lot of time for the seller.

Shelly Walzel: People that may not be qualified and are walking through your home, scoping out how many TVs you have.

Yes, and that's a whole other risk that people need to consider.

So, it's clear why investors work with you and we can see the important part you play within an investor's team.

You are very good at understanding the real estate investor's business. How did you get started with that and what led you to serve investors like you do?

Shelly Walzel: When I started in real estate, I quickly realized how lucrative real estate is. So, I was interested in building my portfolio myself. I was interested in having passive income so I didn't have to work. I had small children and I wanted to be home with them. I was lucky because my husband was very supportive.

I remember coming home one day and saying, "Guess what, honey? I bought two rental houses today." And he said, "Wow, most women buy shoes."

It's very interesting to me how somebody with very little money can become very wealthy in this business. I love seeing it happen and I have seen it happen many times.

I love working with somebody who works hard and really wants to grow a portfolio or a bank account. I love watching them achieve what they want.

I have a lot of good friends in real estate and we sit around and talk business all night long about how we have an idea for this or that. Entrepreneurs are a different breed. They think about things differently. I love that energy. I love the way an idea can become something huge if they think about it long enough or talk about it with a group of like-minded people. I love watching it grow.

Well, it's really obvious that the energy, passion, and commitment you bring to the table for your clients results in a more solid profit and a much greater experience. You help investors not just with their financial well-being, but you also instill the confidence that they have with someone like you on the team.

How can someone find out more about Shelly Walzel and get involved with you if they're a serious investor and ready to make the most of their transactions?

Shelly Walzel: I would welcome anyone to go to my website. It's www.WalzelProperties.com. You can also email me at swalzel@walzelproperties.com.

You can ask me any questions. We can get you in touch with and agent who can help you. We can brainstorm with you and strategize with you and help you get to where you want to be.

About Shelly Walzel

Shelly Walzel has been a licensed real estate professional for over 15 years. She is the Broker/Owner of Walzel Properties, LLC, a real estate brokerage firm in Texas. Walzel Properties currently has over 150 agents that work with investors on a day to day basis closing over $100 million in the past 12 months. She is very familiar with the real estate market and its many quirks. She has been described as a true entrepreneur, having a hard work ethic and being a genius with numbers. She is most known for her ability to see the potential in a specific situation and how everyone can benefit from it. From building rental portfolios to flipping houses to real estate syndications, she is always creative and focused in her approach.

Shelly Walzel is a native Houstonian and has lived in Houston her entire life. She holds a BBA in Business Management from the University of Houston. She has been married to her husband Spencer Walzel for 30 years and has two adult children. All family members are active in the real estate world in one way or another.

Business: Walzel Properties, LLC

Website: WalzelProperties.com

Facebook: Facebook.com/WalzelPropertiesLLC

LinkedIn: LinkedIn.com/pub/WalzelProperties/11/208/430/en

YouTube: YouTube.com/c/WalzelProperties

REAL ESTATE WHOLESALER

Nick Koren is a full-time wholesaler and investor. As one of Houston's top wholesalers, he has been in real estate for over ten years and has wholesaled over a thousand properties in three different major cities. A well-rounded and experienced real estate investor, he also maintains a personal rental portfolio and flips houses as well.

As the general manager and broker of New Western Acquisitions in Houston, he finds wholesale properties that both first-time investors and seasoned real estate investors can buy.

In this interview, Nick discusses the ins and outs of working with a wholesaler. He also breaks down many of the misconceptions some may have about the wholesaling industry with regards to the real estate market.

Nick provides some great insights about how the wholesale process works, in particular using the New Western way. New Western Acquisitions is one of the premier companies to use for purchasing wholesale real estate properties.

Conversation with Nick Koren

Most people don't understand exactly what a real estate wholesaler does, or maybe they have some misinformation or some stereotypes around wholesaling.

What role does a wholesaler play with a real estate investor?

Nick Koren: Essentially, our main focus is to find investment properties for investors. There are many different avenues investors can go to, to find properties and to find deals. Essentially, we like to say we hand the deals to our investors and our customers on a silver platter.

We do a lot of the legwork for them. We negotiate the deals and we get them priced right. Then we present those to investors with all the information that they need to make an educated decision on the purchase of the property.

So wholesaling, in general, is basically presenting those properties to investors so that they don't have to look at a hundred properties in a week. They can look at the three or four that we present to them and then try and make a decision on a deal that's best for them.

You specialize in acquisition and put a lot of resources, both time and money, into marketing and evaluating deals that most people may not have the resources to do.

Many people feel they can use the MLS or go down to the courthouse and buy foreclosures. Are these the strategies that you use to find wholesale properties?

Nick Koren: You're right. People do think that. But those are actually places that we don't focus on.

To touch on the first part, yes, we are a wholesaler. People may think that it is kind of odd in the real estate business but if you think about it, it's the same as any other business where you have a wholesaler - whether it's houses or cars or anything like that. Somebody is out spending the time and money, finding these properties and then putting them in the hands of people who are actually doing the work or fixing them up, selling them or renting them out.

So that is our main focus. We do spend a lot of time and a lot of money out looking and trying to aggressively market for these properties. That is one of the big things that we're able to help people with.

We have a team here of over ten acquisition associates in two locations that do nothing but look for and try to market for investment properties. So if you're an individual trying to buy investment properties, it's hard to cover the same ground we do. If we have ten people out doing that same job, we can find and comb through the deals that won't work and find the ones that do and present those to the potential customers.

If we can look at a hundred deals in a week, an individual may only look at three or four. We're able to comb through those hundreds of deals that are out there and actually find the ones that are really deals. Then we present them to our customers.

We do spend a lot of money, a lot of time and a lot of manpower finding these properties.

While some properties can be found using the MLS, you actually find the hidden gems that don't make their way to the MLS. You go directly to the distressed seller that needs to sell quickly.

Give some examples of the types of sellers you work with and explain why these properties may not be found without the aggressive marketing that you do.

Nick Koren: Most people that are in those situations need to sell quickly. They need to get the cash out of the equity in their house. They need to move on. They may be moving out of state or something like that.

Their perception is that if you list that property on the MLS, you've got to find a real estate agent. You've got to hire a real estate agent. Put the property on the MLS. Get people through the door to try to potentially make an offer on it.

Whereas, we can come in, give them an offer, and say we can close in ten days cash, no questions asked, and they can be on their way. We literally can close in ten days. That's attractive to them because their needs are the cash and they need to move now.

Another example, let's say there's a situation where the house is in really, really bad condition. The reality is if you try to put that on the MLS, you're never going to be able to find an owner occupant buyer for that property because it's never going to qualify for conventional financing.

So they need somebody like us that can pay cash for the house and be able to move quickly and not have to be concerned about the condition of the property.

There are definitely many different scenarios that we come across where people need to sell quickly. But typically, the bottom line is they need to move quickly and they need cash as soon as possible.

Some people may have inherited a house, are behind on taxes, or may be facing foreclosure and don't know what to do.

You create win-win situations for people that normally may have had to walk away from their house or lose their house completely and then you find an investor to use that property in their portfolio.

Nick Koren: Absolutely. In a lot of situations, we've had plenty of people come to us saying, "I'm behind on my payments and the house is going to go into foreclosure."

They may have some equity in that house and their options are to let the bank take it to the auction and sell it and they get nothing. Or sell it to somebody like us that can act quickly, move fast, not worry about financing, buy the property from them and actually put some money in their pocket.

Then, that property goes to an investor that will fix up that property, clean it up, enhance the neighborhood, make some money at the same time and everybody wins.

There are many steps someone would need to do if they were trying to do this on their own.

These might include looking on the MLS, hiring a realtor, sending out postcards, taking out ads and putting up signs. This can be expensive. They would then have to beat someone else to the deal, renovate the property and eventually sell it.

You do all the front-end tasks and just present the contracts to an investor. Is this an accurate representation of what you do as a wholesaler?

Nick Koren: Exactly. That pretty much hits the nail right on the head.

Basically, we're doing the legwork and spending the money and time in order to find those deals.

Again, that goes back to us being able to have a team of people that are out doing this on a daily basis. In this market right now, it's very competitive. The sellers in these situations need somebody quick, somebody fast, to get out there right away.

If you're trying to do this and you're doing the signs and doing the letters and things like that, and you're also trying to run your own business, and maybe rehabbing the houses, and you get a phone call that says, "Hey, I need to sell my house" - can you always get there right away? Or do you have something else that comes up?

That can be the hour or two hours that you can't get out there and somebody else does, and you're going to miss out on that deal.

When somebody calls, you literally can have that deal closed in a matter of an hour or so, right?

Nick Koren: Right. We can get out there and look at it right away. We determine what the needs are for the seller. We cater to whatever it is they need and take care of it right away. That, again, goes back to having a team and having the time and the manpower to make that happen.

A lot of investors, especially new investors, may have heard about wholesalers but they can be hard to find.

What are some of the due diligence steps investors should take before they get into a relationship with a wholesaler?

Nick Koren: The main thing is to ask to see some of the previous properties that they've sold. Also, ask for referrals from other customers that they've worked with.

Then, as far as deal specific, and it's the same in Houston with every wholesaler you're ever going to deal with, you want to do your own due diligence on the property. Wholesalers are going to present you with the price they're asking for it, rehab estimates, after-repair value, things like that.

You need to determine if you're comfortable with those things.

Every investor is different and is going to have certain goals on their return on investment and a certain risk that they're willing to take. Each investor needs to consider that and determine, "Is my risk worth the reward? Is the margin there for my desired profit?"

You cannot just go by what the wholesaler is saying, "Hey, it needs $10,000 or $15,000 in work and it's going to be worth $100,000, $110,000." You need to do your own due diligence to establish that: Yes, I can get the repairs done for this amount and, yes, I feel comfortable with the property because the property can potentially sell for x amount after I fix it up.

Those are the things that you ultimately need to look at and make sure you're comfortable with before you ever sign a contract or make a decision to purchase a property.

Wholesalers act quickly to find and close deals, but your company still closes your properties by the book.

Talk about doing wholesale the right way without unnecessary shortcuts.

Nick Koren: Right. It's not really that it's a short cut. What we do is all by the book. Every property that you're going to purchase from us is going to have a fully insured title. You're going to get free and clear title, so there are no concerns about that.

We're going to be closed by a title company and get a Warranty Deed at the closing.

When you go to an auction, you don't know if you get free and clear title. You're not closing at a title company. You're walking down to the courthouse with cash. You're giving it to the Trustee and then you'll eventually get a deed. Then you have to worry if there is any additional liens or anything like that on the property.

When customers are purchasing from us, it is all done through the traditional avenues. We go through a title company - closing with a title company, getting title insurance and all of that.

One of the reasons why you get so many deals is that you are able to close in cash. However, many of your potential buyers may not be able to pay with cash to purchase from you.

Explain the options people can use to purchase these wholesale properties from you.

Nick Koren: The two main options are cash or hard money.

The conventional financing methods are not going to work with these types of transactions, mainly because the properties are not going to qualify with traditional lenders. And, of course, we are looking to move quicker than they typically move.

So really, your options are cash or hard money. And, again, you're right. A lot of people don't have a lot of cash.

A hard money lender is going to enable you to compete with the cash buyers and close just as quickly.

When a customer comes to us to buy a house, it doesn't matter to us if they're using cash or hard money. They're both the same thing to us and we will take either one of those deals.

If you can get yourself a good hard money lender and build a good relationship with them, that will enable you to close quickly and compete with the cash buyers out there.

Hard money lenders will enable you to get in and get these properties purchased rather quickly.

Quite often, properties can't be sold using traditional means because they don't qualify for financing from a traditional lender.

What are some of the reasons why they would need to be cash or hard money transactions?

Nick Koren: The main reason is the conventional lenders won't lend on these properties. If you go to a traditional big bank and ask them to lend on some of these deals, they're not even interested in them. There may be no carpet on the floor, no kitchen or a hole in the roof. Those are uninsurable properties, so the conventional lenders are not willing to lend on those.

In addition to that, using a hard money lender actually enables the buyers to leverage more of their money. Traditional lenders won't lend nearly as much as a hard money lender will lend on these particular properties. So you actually get to borrow more, which then increases your leverage, and in turn, increases your ROI.

A lot of people that do rentals will purchase a house with hard money. After renovating it, they will go to a traditional lender to refinance it.

What are the out-of-pocket cash implications when they do that versus going conventional?

Nick Koren: If they use a hard money lender and then refinance it to a conventional product, yes, they'll typically end up with less cash out of their pocket, rather than trying to purchase the property directly with conventional financing.

Conventional financing is not going to lend any money to do repairs. Hard money lenders will. So if you can find a conventional lender that will lend on a distressed property, you're still going to have to pay for the repairs out of pocket.

So after you do a refinance, yes, you're typically going to be out of pocket less. Then, when the property is rented and you are getting your cash flow each month, for some people, their ROIs are through the roof. It can be as much as 20%, 30%, 40%, even 50% more with a refinance from a hard money loan.

People often worry about having to make quick decisions on these purchases.

In a wholesale deal, are people able to do due diligence on it prior to making that decision to close?

Nick Koren: We always encourage our customers to do their due diligence. Typically, most of them will bring their contractor with them, any other decision maker's and any additional information that they need to make their decision.

The main thing that most investors are looking for when viewing the properties "What's it going to cost to repair the house?"

So, if an individual can't assess the repairs themselves, they need to bring somebody that can help them.

That's all about building your team. Building the team that you're going to have to help you in your business – wholesalers, contractors, lenders, etc. You need all those people to help you. Having that team is what's going to enable you to make good decisions in a timely manor.

That quick decision is what enables people to get such a great deal. Many people think if they use a real estate agent, they can have a ten-day option period and more time to make a decision.

But, other investors who can decide quickly are also looking at these wholesale properties.

What is the benefit of having a team behind you, if you don't have the knowledge to make a quick decision on your own?

Nick Koren: If you're using a traditional agent, the way the market is right now, as competitive as it is, you're probably not going to get an option period with them either. There are other investors out there that are willing to take that contract without an option period and put down non-refundable earnest money. They just go in there and say, "I'm going to purchase this with cash no contingences" and get the property.

The demand is really high for these properties right now, so you have to build that team to be able to compete and actually get some of these deals that you're looking at.

Some wholesalers might only have a few properties available at any one time.

If someone purchases from you and establishes themselves as a serious investor, what are the advantages of working with your company to find future deals?

Nick Koren: Real estate is a relationship business. Whenever we deal with a customer, we sit down and establish what their goals and expectations are, and what they're trying to accomplish. Then, we present them with properties that fit their needs and their goals.

Because this is a relationship business, one of our agents in our office will work directly with them and will be their point of contact for every property that we get.

Every time we get a property, that agent will contact them via phone and/or email and let them know about the deal. The agent will give the customer the numbers, the property analysis, and set up a time to go take a look at it and personally walk them through the house. Then, they help them make a decision whether or not it's going to work for them.

So it's really a one-on-one relationship. We try to do our best to assess their needs and to try and help them accomplish their goals as best we can.

You're interested in more than just selling properties to sell properties. You take the time to understand an investor's goals.

What do you try to determine in order to help a customer meet those goals?

Nick Koren: We're looking at where they are comfortable purchasing. Houston's a big city so there are plenty of areas. Where are they comfortable investing? Are they looking for flip properties? Are they looking for rental properties?

Are their goals for investing in real estate to get passive income? Is it flips where they're trying to produce the faster money? Are they looking for this to help their rental portfolio for retirement?

What are their goals that they're trying to accomplish? And what are their expectations?

Then we find out how they're going to pay for it. Is it going to be cash? Do we need to get a hard money lender in here to help them pay for that?

Everything is worked out ahead of time so that when there is a deal presented in front of them, they can make a decision quick. We're not giving them a deal that they're not interested in.

You do your best to present customers with properties that are appropriate for their situations and long-term goals so they come back and buy more properties from you. However, you feel strongly that a customer should do his own due diligence.

What are the things people should look at, whether they're working with you or any other wholesaler?

Nick Koren: Right. We provide them with an estimate and it's typically a guide, giving them a general idea for that particular property. They need to do their own due diligence because every investor is different. Every investor has a different vision of what they're going to do with that property.

They need to establish what is going to work for them. Again, every investor has a different return on investment that they're trying to accomplish.

Now, of course, there is a rule of thumb, but everybody's going to be a little bit different. I often use this as an example:

If I have three or four rental properties in a particular neighborhood, and then somebody presents me with a fifth one, that's probably going to be worth more to me than it would to somebody else. Maybe this property makes more sense to me than another property that's clear across town.

So everybody's going to be a little bit different. But, yes, they need to do their own due diligence on the repairs, on what the rental rates are going to be, what the after-repair value is going to be and establish whether or not those numbers are going to work for what their goals are.

That goes back to having that team of advisors and people that are specialists and experts in what they do, to help with that due diligence.

Is there anything we may not have covered for investors that are considering using wholesalers?

Nick Koren: I would say each individual needs to look at their time versus money and determine what works for them. A lot of people have a full-time job and are just looking to do this on the side for an additional income, to add to a retirement portfolio, or things like that.

Really look at what works for you. What's going to be the best use of your time? Spend your time doing what you're most valued at.

Hopefully we can assist you with the real estate side of things and help you find some investment properties that are going to enable you accomplish your goals.

Nick, what is it that led you to this business, becoming a wholesaler and getting as deeply involved in real estate and helping other investors as you do?

Nick Koren: When I grew up, my family had investment properties. Real estate was always of interest to me. The thing that drove me to this side of the real estate business is I would say I'm more of a numbers person. I like the thrill of looking at these numbers, the potential projects and things like that.

Those things got me into the business. What really drives me is seeing other people being able to do that and accomplish their goals. Having success with that and coming back and buying more and more houses. That's what drives me every day to do it again and again. My love and my passion for real estate in general is what got me into it. It's exciting to help other people and see them make money. Then, obviously, they come back and want to buy more properties.

Well, you can certainly see and hear your passion when you share this information.

How can people find out more about Nick and how to get involved with you as a wholesaler, if that's what they're looking for?

Nick Koren: The best thing is to go to www.NewWestern.com. They can look us up on Facebook at New Western Acquisitions. You can connect with me on LinkedIn.com as well.

We'd be more than happy to help you with your real estate goals.

About Nick Koren

General Manager and Broker of New Western Acquisitions-Houston, Nick is full time wholesaler and investor. He has wholesaled well over 1000 properties, maintains a rental portfolio and flips houses as well. Nick has been in real estate for over 10 years in 3 different major cities and has called Houston home for the past 5 years. He has worked with first time investors and seasoned pros in finding and funding their investments. His passion for real estate investing and helping others achieve their goals is what drives him. Above all else he is a devoted husband and father.

Business Name: New Western Acquisitions

Website: NewWestern.com

Facebook: Facebook.com/NewWesternAcquisitionsDallas

LinkedIn: LinkedIn.com/in/HoustonRealEstateInvesting

STEVEN S. NEWSOM

ATTORNEY TO REAL ESTATE INVESTORS

As an attorney who specializes in real estate investment transactions, Steven S. Newsom helps countless real estate investors in the Houston, Texas area.

Steven has found that many investors have a severe lack of knowledge about the complex legal issues surrounding these transactions. Many of these legal issues, when ignored, could result in very costly consequences to the investor.

In this extremely important interview, Steven discusses many of the legal issues investors need to be aware of and what could happen if these issues are ignored. Structuring the contracts, as well as the business entities, in the right way will protect not only the investments, but the investors' personal assets as well.

Rather than being an expense to an investor, an attorney can actually save them money by helping them avoid the problems he discusses in this interview.

Conversation with Steve Newsom

When you watch house flipping shows, you rarely see the attorney or hear them talk about the contracts. That's the stuff that they may not think is exciting to do on those shows. You just see the people buy the house, fix the house, sell the house and cash the check, right?

Steven S. Newsom: Yes. I talk about this a lot, actually, when I talk to real estate investors or when I talk to groups, which I do often.

To me, the legal side is the most neglected part of real estate investing and I also think it's the most important side. Just think, for example, if you buy a house and it turns out it needs $5,000 more in repairs than you thought it did when you inspected it, then you're out $5,000.

But, if you ignore the legal side of it, then you can end up losing the house completely, or you can end up even worse, in a lawsuit which can drag on forever and cost you a ton of money.

I find that a lot of real estate investors, especially those just starting out, don't take the legal side of it seriously. There's not enough education out there about it because, as you said, it's easier to educate people on what type of house to buy: three bedroom, two bath, brick, in a certain price range.

It's difficult, and not necessarily as exciting, to learn about the legal side, but it's even more important than the other.

I tell clients that if you have a choice between checking the title to make sure it's clear and the seller is who they say they are, or looking at the property physically – look at the title. The consequences are so much greater.

I'm amazed how many people that invest in real estate just haven't had the chance or taken the time to learn the basics of the legal side of investing.

That is pretty common – a lot of people don't think about it or look at it.

In real estate, an attorney shouldn't be thought of as an expense. It should be thought of something that saves money.

Texas has some fairly lengthy real estate contracts, even the rental contracts. Many people think there are "standard contracts." Does that even exist, the standard contract?

Steven S. Newsom: Well, they have a standard form of contract for certain deals. For example, the Texas Real Estate Commission has some forms to be used by realtors that are pretty good forms and you can usually just fill in the blanks.

They become non-standard forms when people go in and cross things out or write things in. There's also a space for special provisions where they'll write additional information. So, it's important to note that when the standard contract is changed, it's no longer standard. You need to understand what the changes are.

There are several things I tell people to look out for on a real estate contract.

One is any time anything is crossed out in a contract, such as any of the line items on it, especially in the area where it lists the information that they're going to provide to you. If they cross out something and they say they're not going to give it to you, for example, they're not going to tell you if there are any lawsuits pending related to the property, then you've got to ask yourself why. I would say that's a red flag.

Any time anything is changed, if something is written in, it's really important that they write it in so that it's clear and it can't be misinterpreted.

I have a story about one incident that was really important to one of my clients. She was buying a small apartment complex. When you go to buy an apartment complex, what you do is you look at the cash flow.

The theory is you buy it, you fix it up, you put more renters in there and then the value is higher and your income is better and you can refinance it or whatever.

Well, she was buying it and she couldn't get a loan for enough money to pay what she had to pay to buy it. So the seller agreed that he would do seller financing, and I don't remember the numbers exactly, so I'm going to make this up. Say it was $50,000 for two years until she could get the property fixed up. The problem was that in the contract they wrote, "Seller will take $50,000 owner financing."

My client thought that meant that during the two years all the interest would accrue and she would just make one big balloon payment and wouldn't make any monthly payments. That was important because the cash flow that she was getting on the property changes and she wouldn't have enough money coming in at the beginning to pay him a monthly payment.

So he was sitting across the table from us and I was going through the documents. She got me involved at the very last second, which is not a good idea. So I was just at the closing and I was going through the loan documents, pointing out to her the different terms.

When I got to the loan documents for the seller, it said she was going to be making such and such monthly payments. I told her she was going to be paying this much monthly. She said, "No, there are no monthly payments." The seller sitting across the table from us said, "Yes, there are monthly payments." He thought it meant that she would have to make monthly payments.

It wasn't that either one of them was being a bad guy. It's just that it wasn't written clearly and it made a big difference in this transaction. Luckily, we were able to come to a settlement and we compromised on it.

That could have been a disaster. It was because it was written in that he was going to do this in the special provision section, but it wasn't written clearly.

I have a lot of clients come to me and tell me the contract is too long. They don't want to go to a seller with a twelve-page contract. They want to go with a two-page contract.

The reason the contracts are long is because they address a lot of things that *could* happen. If you don't address those, then you end up with lawsuits. You might end up not getting your earnest money back, or other things like that.

So there are reasons why contracts are long.

The other contracts that you have to look out for are ones that aren't "standard." These are ones that are drafted by attorneys. This happens a lot when you're buying commercial or large apartment complexes. The contracts are custom-made.

We're trained as attorneys to custom draft documents to favor our clients. So, if you ever have a custom-drafted contract, then you want an attorney to look it over.

It also happens if you're ever buying real estate owned properties that are owned by banks or mortgage companies. What they'll do with the "standard" contracts is they will fill out the standard contract and then they'll have "See Addendum A," or whatever they call it. Then, they will attach what is basically a brand new contract that says the standard contract is irrelevant. These are all the terms. Some of those terms can be pretty onerous and it's really important that you look at those very carefully.

So that's why you get an attorney in early so we can look at those things and we can make sure everything's in there.

That's also why you want to use a real contract. It's amazing to me when I see people buying $250,000 houses on a two-page real estate contract. Yes, if everything goes great, it doesn't matter. If everything goes well, you don't need a contract because nobody is going to complain.

The problem is when things go wrong. If you haven't addressed in the contract all the things that can go wrong, which you can't in a two-page contract, then you could end up in a real bind.

Yes, it is critical. A standard contract contains so many blanks that can turn that contract into a very different document.

How many people do you see that just say, "Show me where the lines are, where I need to initial, and let's get this over with?"

Steven S. Newsom: I see that all the time. It's unfortunate because, you're right, if those blanks are not filled out properly or if incorrect selections are made, it can change the transaction tremendously.

Again, it's not necessarily that one party or the other is being the bad guy, it's that they don't have a meeting of the minds.

I teach Contract Law at Rice University and one of the things I hammer all during the entire course is that you have to have a meeting of the minds.

When people are agreeing to the contract, they are both agreeing to the same thing in their minds. If they're not, then you don't really have a contract. So it's very important that things are spelled out properly and blanks are filled in properly so that everybody is on the same page.

That's another important reason to have a written contract. I've had clients come to me that have gotten into partnerships with other people. One guy puts up the money and the other guy does the work. It's very common.

But, they don't even have a written agreement that spells out who is supposed to do what, how much money each owes, or what happens if things go wrong.

And that's the most important thing. If things go right, then you don't need a contract because nobody's going to complain. It's when things go wrong that you need the contract. If you haven't addressed that, you're going to be in big trouble.

I had one client come to me and they had a $550,000 house he was buying with another fellow. The other guy was putting up the money and my client was going to do the physical labor, the sweat equity.

The problem was when the real estate crash hit and things went south. Then, it was a big mess because they didn't have anything that indicated what was going to happen if that happened, if things went south.

You've got to make sure you get all that down.

The other reason to do it is so that we do have a meeting of the minds and so that you understand what is going to happen under certain situations.

One of the things that may be a misconception that people have regarding real estate transactions is they think the title company is handling a lot of their legal issues because the title company is the one that looks at the contract. People assume the title company will see if there are any issues and call if things need clarification.

That really is a big misconception, right?

Steven S. Newsom: Oh, yes. It's a big misconception that a lot of people have.

Let me start off by saying I love title companies. The amount of work they do for what they charge - the insurance, the closing and everything – they're incredible. Most of them are very good and very professional.

I tell all my clients, "I don't care what deal you're in, you need to get title insurance because they do conduct a great search." A lot of people are under a misconception because they don't understand what the title company's role is or they don't understand what title insurance really is and how it works.

They think that the title company is reviewing the contract for me. They're not reviewing the contract to make sure that it says what you thought it said or to make sure that you're getting a good deal.

They're looking at it for specific title-related issues so that they can guarantee it and so that they can issue the insurance. So, no, they're not representing you as far as whether this is a good contract for you or not. They're just looking to see are the names correct and things like that. So, they have a very narrow area that they're looking at.

Sometimes they'll draft the deeds. Usually they contract that out, unless the title company is owned by an attorney. And that's fine. And they may draft a few other documents.

But they're not representing and they're not really giving legal advice to the investor. The investor needs their own attorney to do that.

I guess the other thing I would say is that investors need to understand how title insurance works and they need to be sure and look at the information the title company gives them.

One of the things that happens when you get into a real estate transaction is you go to the title company and the title company will search to make sure and to see what is on the title - liens, easements and things like that.

They'll give you what's called a *Title Commitment*. One of the biggest mistakes that I see real estate investors do is they get this title commitment and they think the title's going to be fine. It's going to be clear because I got this title commitment and they're doing title insurance.

The problem is that's not the way it works. What the title company is doing when they give you that title commitment is they're saying, "Yes, we're going to give you title insurance." And then they're saying, "But we're not going to cover these things." So there are a couple of schedules on the title commitment, Schedule B and Schedule C, where they list the things that are not covered by the title insurance.

That's where things like an IRS lien, a child support lien, a mortgage, a home equity loan or easements that you may not want on there come into play.

You only have a certain period of time during which you can object to things that are on the title commitment and make the seller take them off. If you don't do that, then you may end up buying that piece of property and it may have these other liens or these easements on there.

So, it's critical that investors look at the title commitment. If they don't understand what it says, they need to have somebody look at it. The title company may explain some of it, but they're not acting as an attorney for you so you need to have an attorney look at it.

I had one client, and again, they brought me in late, and this was actually after they discovered the problem. They were going to buy a piece of property to move their high-end car dealership to.

They didn't check the title commitment when they got it and they didn't see there were Homeowner's Association rules and regulations. These HOA rules and regulations covered this piece of property, even though it was commercial.

The problem was that when you read the HOA rules, it specifically said that you could not have a car dealership on the property and that's why they were buying that property.

This was right before closing and the time period they had to object to that and get their earnest money back (which was a lot because it was a commercial piece of property) had passed. They were stuck. Under the contract, they were required to buy that piece of property or lose their earnest money. They couldn't use the property for what they wanted to.

Well, luckily, the property was being sold by a bank, and the bank was very reasonable. We managed to negotiate a settlement that got them their earnest money back and got them out of the deal.

But the bank didn't have to do that. They could have been hard line and they could have just said, "Forget it." Or, "We have a contract and you have to buy the property and we get to keep your earnest money." But, again, after I talked to them for a while, they were reasonable.

So it's very important that people look at the title commitment. Most people don't understand how it works.

You definitely brought up an important fact so people can see it's a completely separate part of the legal puzzle that comes along with the transaction.

You also mentioned, when you were talking about partnerships, how one person puts up the money and the other person does the work. One of the first questions that a lot of people have when they first get into investing in real estate is How should I establish my company?

Do I buy these in my name? Do I run my business out of an LLC or a corporation? What are the different pieces of legal documents? Obviously, whether they have an LLC or a corporation, there still needs to be some kind of agreement on how that's run.

A lot of people don't understand the separation of company formation from the legal standpoint to the financial or the tax standpoint, right?

Steven S. Newsom: Yes. It's a very critical decision to make. I suggest to all of my clients, especially the ones that are relatively new to real estate, that don't have a lot of experience running companies, that the best thing to do for most real estate investors is to form a Limited Liability Company, an LLC.

Now, one of the things that comes up a lot, because you hear things on TV and gurus talk about set it up this way or whatever, is where to form the LLC. A big part of my business is helping people form their companies and I do an incredible number of those.

One of the things that they ask is, "Where do I form it?" They'll tell me that some guru told them, "You want to form a Nevada corporation or a Delaware one." Or, "You want a Nevada corporation owned by a Delaware corporation owned by a land trust or whatever."

Then they set up these really complicated schemes. The only reason to do that is they think that if you make it hard for somebody to find out who the owner is, then they can't sue you. I laugh at them and say, "In today's world, I will find you. If I'm an attorney and I have a client that's been injured on your property, I don't care how many layers you've gone through. I'm going to find you."

In Texas, when you form an LLC, the names of the owners or the managers are public because they're in the filing. So that's how they can find you.

But, if you form it in, for example, Nevada, those names are not made public. My response to that is, "I'll find you because I'll just subpoena the Nevada Secretary of State and they'll have to tell me. So you can't hide anymore."

I've had clients that have come to me that spent thousands of dollars on these schemes. They've set up different companies to just try to hide who they are.

The other thing is you've got to look at this from a practical standpoint, too. If I get you into court and you set up all these weird corporation entities, I'm going to get up there and I'm going to tell the jury. I'm going to ride it out and I'm going to show the jury this network of companies. I'm going to turn to you and ask, "Why did you do that?" And the only answer is, "To hide."

Well, I just won the case no matter what the facts are because the jury is not going to like you because you're being sneaky. Juries don't like sneaky people.

So it's important that they do set something up, but they need to set it up properly for the reasons I just mentioned.

Now, what do they set up? I like the LLC because it's the simplest to use, it's the most flexible to use and it provides you with liability protection.

The interesting thing about liability protection is that it actually works in two ways. Most people understand that a corporation or an LLC will provide liability protection if something happens at the property and there's a lawsuit brought against the property and you have it under one of these companies. Typically, only the stuff that's in the company would be at risk, unless you did something yourself. For example, if you walk over and you punch the tenant in the nose, well, you're really personally liable, in addition to the company.

But, if it's something that has to do with the property, it will protect your other personal assets. That's great, and that's the biggest reason to form the LLC.

The other thing that a lot of people don't realize is it protects the LLC from you. You could be out driving around in your car and get in a car accident that has nothing to do with your rental properties and get sued for $10 million. Your insurance will cover whatever your cap is. Say you've got really good car insurance and your cap is a million dollars. Well, now you're on the hook for $9 million because your insurance won't pay that.

So what does the attorney for the plaintiff do? They look to see what assets you have. Now, they'd love to get at those rental properties. But if you have them in an LLC, they can't get them. What they can get is something called a charging order, which means if the LLC distributes any money out to you, then they can try and attach that if they can catch it.

But they can't get any management power for the LLCs. So what do you do? You just don't ever distribute anything. You pay for your health insurance inside the company. You drive a company car. You just use all your money inside the company. You don't distribute it out. So they can't get it.

It's even better than that. It's like a poison pill because when it comes to taxes, what will happen is if the LLC makes any income, depending on how you selected to have it taxed, then that creditor who has the charging order giving them the right to distributions, may have a tax liability but not be able to get any of the money to pay it.

It makes it very difficult for creditors to break through that. So LLCs are the greatest things since crunchy peanut butter because they're so flexible and they give you that liability protection.

You provided some great insights for people considering LLC, corporations, and S corps.

When you form an LLC, that just forms the shell of the company. If you have more than one person, like partners, the LLC doesn't necessarily define the terms of that partnership, correct?

Steven S. Newsom: Yes. And there are a couple of ways to do it.

One is if you're forming an LLC to do the transaction, the partners are both owners of the LLC. And in the LLC, there are certain documents you have to have. One of them is an operating agreement. And in the operating agreement is where you'll define who gets what and who has to do what. So it's a critical document to have.

One of the big mistakes that I see people do with forming companies is they'll go to their accountant or their CPA or they'll go online to one of these services to form the LLC. All they'll do is file the form with the Secretary of State. That's just the first step and the easiest step.

You also have to have an Operating Agreement, as well as several other documents you're required to have. If you don't have them, then when you get to court, one of the things they'll try and do is they'll try and break that liability protection.

One of the things they'll look at is if you have an Operating Agreement. Did you issue your member certificates? All those things you're supposed to do. And a lot of my clients come to me later and they'll say they didn't know they had to have all that stuff.

So it's important that they have that. And that's also where you have the definitions of who's going to do what, and who's going to get what, so it's critical to have it.

There are a lot of different ways to structure it. You can have them together in the same LLC. You can have each in a separate LLC that has an agreement between them. It always depends on the circumstances of each transaction, which a lot of times are different, but it's critical to do that.

One of the things I'll mention also is when you don't do your transactions in an entity. Say you and I got together. You were going to give me the money and I was going to go buy a house and fix it up. We're now partners under the law, even if we don't have a partnership agreement.

So let's say you don't even have a partnership agreement. One of the big problems with not having an entity involved is that if I'm driving over to the property to collect the rent or do some maintenance and I get in a car accident, I'm on partnership business. You're liable for my actions as my partner. So you could end up being liable for the car accident I got into, or the fight I got into with the tenant, or whatever.

Again, if you're going to go into a partnership with somebody, you have to understand that you're picking up a liability, unless you're in an entity, which will limit that liability and it's a big deal.

It's almost like putting a sign out without having a store behind it. If anything really happened, that would be a very weak barrier because of how they set it up.

Steven S. Newsom: That's right. It would be much weaker than if they did it right. That is a big mistake a lot of people make. They don't follow through and do all the documents they need.

Another thing is these online services charge them so much. I'm amazed what people pay, sometimes, to get these LLCs formed. People think attorneys are expensive. I look at some of these costs that people pay. I've had people tell me they've paid $1500 or $2000 for a one-person LLC, plus they didn't get all the stuff they needed.

I had one client that actually did one of these online LLCs and he was told they had formed the company, but he never got any documents and he operated for over a year, assuming he had a company. Actually, they had never filed it.

So, I just think it's dangerous. It's not that expensive. If you're going to do it, just do it properly.

"Penny wise and pound foolish," that's the way I think a lot of people think of attorneys. I tell people you can pay me a little bit now to do it right, or you can pay me a lot later to fix it.

Just like with a doctor, it's going to cost you a lot less to go through a prevention plan than it is to find a cure.

That's where a lot of people find themselves backed into a corner. The attorneys don't take advantage of people because they're backed into a corner, they just have a big mess to deal with at that point that they may have been able to avoid before.

Steven S. Newsom: That's right.

You also work with investors that invest in real estate notes. These are investors that are playing the part of a bank where they're lending money out.

An investor or a person buying a home may normally go to a mortgage company or a hard money lender for real estate, but instead they're actually going to a private individual that has funds, whether it's savings or an IRA.

Talk a little bit about the people that are lending money on real estate and some of the things they need to consider.

Steven S. Newsom: The most important thing for them is to make sure that they protect the principal, the money that they're loaning out. I do a lot of private loan packages, which is a collection of documents you need to protect those monies.

You protect it by having the documents drafted properly and by making sure that they're secured by the property. So one of the things that a lot of lenders don't have is an attorney that knows how to do that.

With investors, you often get a lot of pretty straightforward contracts. They usually pay a high interest rate for a short period of time, such as six months to two years, and that's to buy the property and to fix it up.

So a lot of my clients will loan that bridge financing to the investor so they can do that. Then once the property's fixed up and it's worth more, the buyers can either sell it or they can go get traditional financing.

The key is to make sure your documents are drafted properly. Investors sometimes come up with unusual or different schemes. They'll have a first lien and a second lien. Or, they'll have a first lien and owner financing, things like that.

Sometimes they'll have a special requirement. The payments have to be made not on the 1st, but on the16th. So there are all kinds of different things that can change and you need to make sure that those are all drafted in the contracts properly.

That's what I do a lot of. It's an important part of the real estate investing industry that a lot of people don't even realize is out there. There are a lot of people who loan out of their IRAs or their savings because they can make a lot more money. Also, they're secured by real estate, which is, I think, much safer than the stock market or stocks or bonds.

People have lost confidence in traditional investing and they don't make any money with their CDs. So it's a good option for people that want to loan money. It's relatively safe if it's done properly.

That's one of the true benefits of working with an attorney, but also working with an attorney like you that is extremely knowledgeable and laser-focused on real estate and the ins and outs of real estate and its intricacies. You really help people navigate through those problems.

What is it that led you to do this and serve the types of clients you serve? Not just in your practice, but also the real estate workshops where you're educating people.

Steven S. Newsom: Well, a couple of things. One, I've always enjoyed teaching so that's why I teach at Rice University. That's why I give these seminars and workshops.

And I noticed, because I've been a real estate investor myself in the past, that there just wasn't very much good information out there on the legal side. There were a lot of misconceptions being taught that weren't true.

One of the things, for example, that I ran into a lot was I would hear people say, "You don't really need to form an LLC for your properties until you have five or ten properties. And then you can do it."

That just didn't make any sense to me at all. What if you get sued on the third house you buy? Well, then it's too late. So, the misconceptions bugged me.

I've always been interested in real estate. Actually, I've been a real estate investor myself. Law is my third career. I was an engineer, then I got my MBA and had a company that taught classes for people who were starting small businesses and consulted with them. Finally, I got my law degree. I kind of carried over that same mindset of real world practical stuff, which I didn't see in a lot of legal information that was being given to people.

I also have the desire to teach people because I try to keep them out of trouble.

It's also a very creative thing. Many real estate transactions are the same. But, there is a lot of creativity in what we can do with real estate investments and how you can structure things. Helping with that really interests me.

It's also a positive thing. When you go and you teach somebody what these contracts really mean and how they are and you keep them out of trouble, you're really doing something positive. When you help people figure out how they can make a transaction work so it helps everybody, that's a positive thing versus when I used to do litigation (which I don't do anymore), it was very negative.

So that's how I got to where I am and I've got this focus and this narrow practice of helping real estate investors, especially the new and the small real estate investors. When I say smaller, I've had clients that have bought $35 million apartment complex portfolios and then I've had clients that buy $80,000 single family homes.

It's the transaction that I really work with and there are really not a lot of people focused on helping the independent smaller investors. So that's the niche that I've filled. In addition, I like dealing with the people.

Real estate investors represent a wide range of people. You meet all kinds of interesting people and characters and so that can be fun, too.

That's one of the reasons that you are a true educator and an advocate for the success of your clients and real estate investors. You're a tremendous person to have on this important real estate team.

How can people find out more about Steve Newsom, especially if they're in Texas doing real estate?

Steven S. Newsom: It's easy to contact me. Either call me at 281-829-2074 or shoot me an email at snewsom@sbcglobal.net.

About Steven S. Newsom

Steve Newsom is a general Civil Practice attorney who focuses on real estate, business, and contract law. He assists clients with purchasing and selling real estate, foreclosures, title issues, evictions, loan applications, and drafting loan packages for lenders.

In addition, he helps businesses form entities and utilizes creative finance methods such as "wrap" sales for real estate. Steve also manages legal issues related to raising funds to invest in real estate, including the preparation of private placement memoranda.

Steve shares his real estate knowledge through seminars on a wide range of legal topics. He also teaches Contract Law and other legal topics for the Paralegal Certification Program at Rice University.

Contact Steve via email at snewsom@sbcglobal.net.

LENDER

As the president of Capital Concepts, Blake A. Yarborough excels in finding different lending strategies in the real estate investing world.

Traditional lending options often fall short when real estate investors are trying to purchase one or more properties. Blake's creativity and persistence in searching out alternative lenders have given him the reputation as the person to seek out in the Houston area.

Blake doesn't just find loans for other people. He lives and breathes real estate investing as he continues to grow his own portfolio. Whether it's an up or down market, Blake has been there, done that, and can help others navigate the lending marketplace to make a purchase happen.

He not only helps others find loans for properties they're interested in buying, but he also advises them as to the best strategies to use, such as a double close technique. This involves not only having cash flow, but equity as well, which can often provide a positive exit strategy.

Conversation with Blake Yarborough

Blake, you're the guy a lot of real estate investors come to for money to purchase properties. These are investors who are buying and flipping, and also investors that are in it for the long haul to create a real business with monthly income.

A lot of people think of a mortgage as a debt. You separate debt into two categories: bad debt and good debt. Explain the difference between those two categories.

Blake A. Yarborough: When I talk about good debt and bad debt, good debt is debt that produces an income. Basically, you buy something that's giving you more cash flow than the debt costs and it's a net positive.

Bad debt is like a car loan or credit cards and also your house mortgage. These are money outflows, whereas good debt is money inflow.

You're saying when people use mortgages and borrow money to purchase real estate, they shouldn't look at that as that's where my money's going. They should look at it as that's where my money's coming from, right?

Blake A. Yarborough: Right. It's producing an income.

If we have properly financed properties, we can really maximize the cash on cash returns by appropriately using leverage to produce the cash flow goals that we're looking for.

Talk about the typical investor that you work with who borrows to buy rental properties. What are some of the misconceptions they have about borrowing money to fund and build up a portfolio? And what is the outcome they seek to achieve?

Blake A. Yarborough: One of the biggest misconceptions comes from most brokers out there only offering one type of loan. And on investment properties, people also think they need to put 20% or 25% down. Or that if they own more than four properties, they can't buy more.

People need to realize a conventional loan is only one type of loan and you can use synergy for multiple types of loan products.

For instance, with hard money loans, you may buy a property with as little as $1,000, $2,000 or $3,000 out of pocket and then you can immediately refinance that into a conventional loan. In those situations, you may have 100% cash on cash returns.

So it's really about learning how to use the synergies between the multiple types of loan programs and, of course, find the property you want.

You've personally been through several different market ups and downs in the Houston area. There were times when it was easy to buy properties and then things crashed. Some people kept investing through those times and they seem to have come out and built a nice portfolio.

When people borrow money by leveraging that good debt, how does that help them go through those good times and bad times within the real estate market?

Blake A. Yarborough: During the heydays, when everybody was getting loans if you could just sign and drive, the underwriting guidelines had gotten a little bit too lax.

Then we had the market bubble burst and we had an overreaction and they pulled back the guidelines too far. We went from everybody could get a loan to people couldn't get a loan. And now, we're starting to loosen up again.

By properly financing these properties, it can give you additional income during a down period to help protect your family, just in case you lost a job or something along those lines. It's about security. It's about providing peace of mind where you can spend time with your family if you do have enough income coming in from these properties.

The other thing I want to touch on is, as I said before, the guidelines for conventional financing got so tight from an overreaction. People need to know there are other types of loans. As long as you've taken care of your credit, you've been responsible with acquiring more debt, and you're buying a good property, there are other portfolio-type lenders that will lend to you.

I really struggle to explain to people that there are so many types of loans available. You might not qualify for this loan or that one's unavailable at this time, but then we can look at Plan B.

I think one of the biggest tools I have and one of the largest ways I can help people is by showing them the different products that are available to them.

You're not just as a lender. You're also an investor and you've been through the ups and downs like everyone else.

You're known as someone who goes out and finds unique loan products and tools that give people those options you talk about. How did that come about?

Blake A. Yarborough: The last six years, my lending has always following my personal investing. When I outgrew Fannie Mae, I started dealing with local banks or portfolio lenders and got to know hedge fund lenders because I needed loans for myself.

Once I found these loan programs or lenders, I sent the roadmap to my clients. These people can do this. Let me help you get that loan. That's why I have one client who I've done over twenty loans for in the last five or six years because they can keep on growing with my help. As they grow their investment portfolio, I continue to research to find lenders to provide those loans for them.

Now, you don't just fill out paperwork for people to push loans through. You actually see what the deal looks like and you have a pretty keen sense of what will go through and you act as that advisor.

Have you helped investors recognize a potentially bad deal and maybe saved them a lot of stress and heartache?

Blake A. Yarborough: One of the values of having someone like me on your team is having that second set of eyes. I have opinions about financing real estate and buying investment properties. One of the reasons why I always use the double close technique is for leverage. Another reason is that it forces you to buy with equity. If you buy with enough equity, you should have cash flow as long as you stay under a certain threshold, depending on the area.

One of the biggest mistakes I see people make is buying property just to buy it. If you buy a property and it doesn't have any equity and you get in a pinch and you have to turn around and sell it, you'll lose money. And people don't want to lose money.

So if you buy with equity and cash flow, you may never want to sell it because it's providing an income. If you have to sell it, at least you'll make some money.

So that's why I like doing the double close technique, because it forces you to buy with equity and cash flow. One of the biggest mistakes people make is when they say I'm buying this one which has a lot of cash flow and yet, there is no equity if they have to turn around and sell it and pay fees, etc.

A lot of people think they need to put 20% down to buy investment properties. How many people feel that 20% down is a good equity in case something comes up?

Blake A. Yarborough: Well, Bill Gates may want to put 20% down and as long as that rate of return works for him, it's okay.

But most of the clients I see, and most of the general population out there, need to maximize their cash on cash returns and the returns they're using with their limited amount of resources.

So it depends on people's situations. I really feel that if you maximize it, then you can make large differences in your portfolio over time.

If somebody puts 20% down plus closing costs plus they paint and carpet it, depending on the bill, it may cost them $25,000 or $30,000 to buy one house. But with that same amount of money when I was first buying, I bought eight houses with $32,000 out of pocket using the double close technique, and hard money loans to refinance later. The cash flow from eight houses is obviously better than the cash flow from one house.

A lot of people start their investment portfolio with a single-family home. But you've seen people grow and change course dramatically.

In fact, you have invested in a wide variety of properties yourself.

What other types of properties do you invest in and also help folks get financing for?

Blake A. Yarborough: Personally, I have roughly a hundred houses, plus some small apartments. As I stated earlier, a lot of my lending has followed my personal investing. So now I offer loans for smaller commercial properties, like small apartments and storage. I'm also starting to look at some development deals, but that's just where I am as an investor.

So it's not just the one or a few houses. As a person grows and maybe sells off their properties and becomes ready to move up to a bigger property, we can help them as well.

You started out lending and you built up a reputation for helping real estate investors, then you took the dive in yourself.

What was it like when you first started? You talked about those eight houses that you bought. Were those the first houses that you purchased?

Blake A. Yarborough: Yes. Technically, I had one house years before, but that's it. Basically, it happened at the end of '08. I looked at my wife and I wasn't sure if my mortgage business was going to survive. It was a tough time for everybody with the economy. I had a 3-year-old daughter and a 1-year-old son and I wasn't sure how I was going to make it.

I'd been financing all these other people and I thought let me finance my own. I started out buying ten houses and twelve doors over a six-month period and it produced roughly $5,000 a month in cash flow.

My wife was trying to go back to being a dialysis nurse at the time and she noticed what the cash flow would be once I refinanced. She immediately went from being a dialysis nurse to being a property manager.

That was an epiphany for us. It allowed us to raise our own children, instead of putting them in daycare. We've just been growing that portfolio ever since.

That's really amazing. A lot of people think that real estate is something that they're going to grow into over years. But you found your back against the wall and you created a $5,000 a month income in six months, which a lot of people could live on.

What is that cash flow now? Do you still have those in your portfolio?

Blake A. Yarborough: Absolutely. We still have every one of those houses and I think right now it's up to about $5,500 or $5,600. The portfolio is ten times larger now with substantially more cash flow!

Purchasing real estate is an emotional decision, and when people are buying their first property, many are afraid.

Do you see a fear of failure and what you also call a fear of success, as people move closer to going from "I'm going to be a real estate investor" to "I am a real estate investor"?

Blake A. Yarborough: It's funny because you'll see people be nervous buying their first property. And then you'll see people that have twenty properties that have the same nervousness when jumping into a small multi-family.

In both cases, these people may have the right team in place and it's just that they're afraid to take that step out of their comfort zone.

But once they do that, with the right team around them, they feel this is okay and it works for them. Once they start taking action, usually it's all downhill from there.

Once you start doing it, then it becomes easier and easier.

Smart investors choose to work with team members who are going to help them achieve the outcome they want, even if their services cost more.

What are some of the mistakes real estate investors make when it comes to financing? Have you seen people make decisions based on someone offering lower points or things like that?

Blake A. Yarborough: A couple of things come to mind when you start talking about that.

I used to do business with Brant. One of the reasons why I did a lot of business with Brant is because I trusted it would be done correctly and it freed me up for doing my mortgage job.

As far as clients coming to me for mortgages, it's the old saying - tripping over pennies, running for dollars. Yes, there is always going to be a lower-priced person out there but it really comes down to the quality of advice you receive.

The other thing that comes to mind is why do they have to discount it so much? Are they lacking in customer service? Or are they lacking in knowledge? They're treating their product like a commodity. And that's what some people are looking for.

But when it comes to financing an investment property, I believe knowing about all the tools you have to use in each situation is vitally important. And most of the conventional lenders don't have that.

Or don't know about it. One of the big things is you only learn about the options that they can provide.

Blake A. Yarborough: Everybody's going to sell what they have to sell.

Right. You're very involved in the real estate investment community in Houston and you speak at a lot of events, educating people on the big picture and the principles.

What is the biggest mistake a real estate investor will make right now?

Can you give us an apples to apples example of what it might look like if someone did something one way versus the other way by not knowing an option is available?

Blake A. Yarborough: To address something you mentioned earlier, it comes down to education. If you really have sought out learning from somebody that's qualified to teach real estate investment, they will lay out many of the different areas and techniques, including everything from property management to rehabbing the property to financing the property.

And that brings us to having the proper team.

As far as somebody coming in with the wrong financing information, there's an old saying. Anytime you think you've been screwed over in business, it's for one of two reasons. You're too greedy or too lazy.

If you're too greedy, you've lost because of an eighth of a point or you didn't get the proper advice.

The other way you lose is if you were too lazy. You didn't do the research or you didn't do the validation.

If you feel like you're been messed over in real estate, most likely it's for one of those two reasons.

As far as somebody not opening their mind to certain loan products that have a temporary high interest rate, that limits their possibilities for financing more and more properties and really growing their portfolio. As I touched on earlier, if you're Bill Gates, then you can do that.

But I have found that most people don't have the bank account Bill Gates has and if you start putting $20,000 or $30,000 down on each property, some people with a lot of money may buy ten or fifteen properties.

But what if you're able to take that same money and buy a hundred properties? I think when I was at 50 or 60 properties, at that point, I had just under $190,000 invested.

Whereas in that scenario of people putting $20,000 down, you may have only bought ten houses. I'll let any investor choose. I know which one they will choose.

That is remarkable. So if someone has $30,000, there are a vast array of things they can do with it. And these are options that a lot of people either neglect or are not informed about.

Is there anything else that you wanted to mention?

Blake A. Yarborough: Real estate has done wonders for my life in the last six years. There is nothing that can build wealth faster than real estate.

The way I look at real estate is that every house I buy has a little cash flow and it's like a savings bank. The power or the confidence it gives you is very powerful when you build a portfolio up and you know that at any time you can sell those properties, pay off a very expensive house and still have plenty left in a portfolio.

One of the things I mention when I do some of my presentations is if someone makes $30,000 a year, how long would it take him to save $30,000? It would take him a long time. But if we showed him how to buy one house, he might save $30,000 overnight just by buying that house.

Or let's say he lives in a hundred thousand dollar house. And he bought three investment properties. He could sell those three investment properties at any time and pay off his new residence.

What that would do for that one individual is life changing. I just broke that down to a small scale, but that's essentially what it's done for me. And that's the piece of the pie or the dream that I want to share with as many people as I can because it truly is life-changing.

It certainly sounds it. And one of the biggest things is it gives you choices. That's something that a lot of people don't have the luxury of having and it's something that really creates peace of mind.

That's why you're part of this Real Estate Dream Team because of your ability to share the opportunities that people may not find in other places. You've certainly changed the lives of a lot of people.

How can people find out more about Blake Yarborough and Capital Concepts?

Blake A. Yarborough: They can check us out online at www.4SmartMoney.com or call us toll free at 877-651-9500.

About Blake A. Yarborough

Blake A. Yarborough is a Houston native who graduated in 1995 with a MBA from University of St. Thomas with concentrations in Finance & Marketing. He is the President of Capital Concepts, Inc., a company that he started in 1998. Blake became a Real Estate Professional in 1996. He also has been a Mortgage Broker since 1998. Blake has a background in securities & insurance, and is a Real Estate Investor as well.

Blake is an Investor, Speaker/Presenter & Frequent Radio Expert. Blake is a licensed Certified Financial Planner, Real Estate Broker, Mortgage Broker/Banker & Hard Money Lender.

As an investor, Blake is looking for the programs that investors are seeking. He has conventional financing, hard money, blanket loans, bank portfolio loans and Commercial Loans! He has loans for more than 4, 10 or even 50 properties! He currently has a rental portfolio of more than 100 properties himself since Nov 2008 and continues to purchase more properties via programs Capital Concepts, Inc. & Investor Lending, LLC have available! He is an expert at using

Financing Techniques & Programs to accelerate peoples RE Investing Goals. He can teach you to look at your deal and find the ideal program for your situation, depending on your intentions with the property.

Business Name: Capital Concepts, Inc.

Website: 4SmartMoney.com

Facebook: Facebook.com/4SmartMoney

LinkedIn: LinkedIn.com/pub/Blake-Yarborough-cfp-cam-caps/1/856/790

YouTube: YouTube.com/user/CapitalConceptsLoans

PRIVATE FINANCING THROUGH SELF-DIRECTED IRAS

H. Quincy Long is the president and founder of Quest IRA, Inc. He is incredibly knowledgeable about financing, especially having to do with real estate investing.

His company helps investors not only grow their retirement or investment portfolios, but also provides the opportunity for those who want to lend money to connect with those who need money in the real estate niche.

Quest IRA is one of the leading self-directed IRA providers in the country. Self-directed IRAs are normally used to invest in alternative investments. Real estate and notes are popular investments to use with these IRAs.

As a real estate investor himself, Quincy shares many creative strategies he has used with his own self-directed IRAs, as well as strategies others have used to grow their IRAs and portfolios.

His seminars and workshops not only help to educate those who want to learn about using this important tool, but also serve as networking venues for those who want to meet others who are using self-directed IRAs as an investment tool. Buyers and sellers of houses, as well as people that lend money to investors for real estate, all benefit from Quincy's knowledge and his company's resources.

Conversation with H. Quincy Long

What makes self-directed IRAs special?

H. Quincy Long: A self-directed IRA is a very flexible tool. There is a lot of flexibility in what you can invest in with these IRAs – not just the little box of stocks, bonds, mutual funds and annuities.

You have two different groups of people that look at you as someone that can make a big difference in their business.

The first group of people have IRAs. They've saved money through company retirement plans and IRAs.

What's the reality of the flexibility of that retirement account, the savings that they worked so hard to accumulate?

H. Quincy Long: The flexibility there is that most people think you can only invest in stocks or mutual funds or annuities or bonds. But why do they think that? The answer is simple. That's what the stock, mutual fund and annuity companies want you to think.

The truth of the matter is an IRA can invest in many different types of investments. There are very few restrictions contained in the Internal Revenue Code.

IRAs can and do invest in real estate itself, promissory notes (sometimes secured by real estate and sometimes not), options, oil and gas ventures, privately held stock, limited liability companies, limited partnerships, trusts and a whole lot of other stuff that you wouldn't even think typically would go into an IRA.

So that's one aspect of it.

Many people do wish there was something else they could do besides the stock market and mutual funds.

Describe what Quest is and how Quest facilitates things for people when they make the decision to take control of their savings and their IRA and make these self-directed investments.

H. Quincy Long: We call ourselves the premier Self-directed IRA provider in the country. Basically, our function is in some ways limited, but our function is to hold non-traditional assets in IRAs and allow people the freedom to invest in what they know best.

In order to help people do that, we provide a lot of free education on the restrictions and the benefits of what you can do with a Self-directed IRA and also networking opportunities in all of our offices.

We educate people, but ultimately the investor – the IRA owner – does have to make their own decisions about how they invest their money. That's the double-edged sword of a Self-directed IRA.

The good news is that it is self-directed and you get to invest in what you know and understand best. The bad news is that it is self-directed and you have to invest in something that you know and understand or you're likely to have problems.

So we're a neutral holder of non-traditional assets in IRAs.

The reason so many people use Quest to actually achieve financial freedom is the fact that it's a place where they can do self-directed investments.

Some people may think you're like a brokerage but you're not because you don't ever guide them towards one investment or the other and you don't even evaluate investments.

H. Quincy Long: That's right. The accounts are self-directed. But the beauty is that we do provide so much education and networking opportunities that we think are so important for our clients' success.

When I was first starting the idea of Quest IRA, two friends and I got together and we said, "We have Self-directed IRAs. And they're fun but it's a lonely world, unless you know other people with Self-directed IRAs and you can do deals with each other and stuff like that."

So we started a little group that we called Inet to get together and discuss Self-directed IRAs. We did that for a couple of years before I started Quest IRA. I really learned how I wanted to run Quest IRA. I wanted to give people the education to use this very powerful tool and provide them networking and educational opportunities. And that's what I've done.

The networking opportunities that you talk about are so important because there are people that have learned about the opportunities to use this money to invest in real estate and gone through the process of moving their money into a Self-directed IRA.

Then they hit a wall of "Who can I lend this to?" You have two groups of people that desperately want to find each other but seem to keep missing each other throughout the country.

What's an estimated amount of money that people have sitting dormant in self-directed IRAs at your company because they haven't found a place to invest it yet?

H. Quincy Long: Yes, I actually do have a pretty good idea of that. Let's just say it's in excess of $100 million.

That's staggering.

Many of your clients with self-directed IRAs offer a type of lending that's called 'private money.' The other group of people you work with and educate are real estate investors who are looking for this non-traditional funding for their deals.

Many people think those are people that don't have good credit or they can't get money anywhere else. That's not the case. These are solid investors that need alternative financing because they may have hit a limit with traditional financing or with banking institutions.

Talk about how you educate real estate investors.

H. Quincy Long: One of the things I mentioned that people can do with Self-directed IRAs is loan money secured by real estate. In other words, purchase promissory notes or create promissory notes.

Since people can make loans secured by real estate, they need to find the people that want to borrow that money. So at our networking events, we have a lot of opportunities for people to meet each other.

We'll give a class, for example, on private lending. After the class, people stand up and introduce themselves. You always have to do your own due diligence with anybody you meet anywhere, and there's no difference with Quest IRA because we don't recommend investments or investors.

There have been people at Quest IRA that have raised literally into the tens of millions of dollars for their real estate investment career over the last several years through networking with people who have self-directed IRAs.

I can think of one client who heard about the idea of private financing through a self-directed IRA, and she wondered if she could buy a house with literally no money out of her pocket.

She found a good house that she could buy at a good price. It needed very little repairs, maybe $5,000 worth of work. She had heard about a friend of hers who was retiring from a company and was rolling his former company's 401k account into an IRA.

She helped him to understand that he could roll it into a self-directed IRA at Quest IRA. Then, he made a loan to her to acquire that property and she had no money out of her pocket for this property to be a rental in her portfolio. That's just one example.

That's a perfect example of the flexibility. When a lot of people go through traditional financing, there is generally a structure and a formality that everything has to go through.

But private money is a relationship-based business. When it comes down to setting terms, whether it's interest rates, how long the terms are or what the payback terms are, the sky's the limit on what that is, and it's really based more on that relationship than any other predetermined guidelines.

H. Quincy Long: Of course. My typical loans out of my retirement plan are a couple of points and 12%. That's not real hard money nor is it real soft money. They're typically a year-long loan.

But I'm very flexible. I've loaned money at a lower interest rate, such as 10% and 1 point. And I've seen clients lend money as low as 6% or 7% to someone that they know and trust where there's a "bird's nest on the ground" loan, where the loan to value is very low so they feel very safe.

You can do tremendously creative things. We have people, including myself, who have done equity participation loans to lower the cost during the loan term, in exchange for a little bit of the upside when the investor sells the property.

Both clients and I have structured deals where the financing is provided by the IRA for the investor to buy the property, and then the investor wraps the IRA's first-lien loan with a wrap-around loan to a new buyer. I feel very secure in this situation, because I've got a wrap-around lender behind me to make sure that my loan performs. There are an unending variety of things you can do with private financing in a Self-directed IRA.

You've probably seen firsthand more creative financing strategies and techniques than probably anyone that I can think of in the real estate financing business in the last hundred years.

What would be one example of those creative things that you've seen that most people would say, "You can do that?"

H. Quincy Long: Well, some of the things I've done recently myself have been very interesting.

Say that an investor needs cash to buy a property, and then they're going to sell it with seller financing. Normally you can get substantially more for a house if you provide the financing for it, but of course it ties up your funds. I've done some very interesting things to solve that problem for the investor, while getting a very secure loan for my retirement account. For example, I recently did a deal on a duplex in

Indiana, and I've done some similar deals in Mississippi, as well. But in Indiana, the investor said he needed $10,000 to buy a property for cash. Before he closed, he found a buyer for the property for $36,999 with $2,000 down and a first-lien loan for $34,999 at 9.99% interest and 120 payments of $462.32 each. The investor didn't want to put his own money up to buy the property.

The solution was to arrange for a buyer to buy the property at the same time that he buys it from the current owner. To raise the cash to get the deal done, the investor sold my IRA (actually it was my Self-directed Health Savings Account) the first 54 payments of the note for $18,075.11 at a yield to my account of 15%.

So what did that do? The investor got to purchase the property without any cost out of his pocket, and in fact he was able to put more than $10,000 in his pocket between my purchase of part of the note and the new buyer's down payment. At the same time, it got my account an income stream of 54 payments of $462.32 at a yield of 15%. I feel totally secure knowing that the investor will make sure those payments get made so that he will receive the remaining 66 payments on the note. Finally, the end buyer of the duplex got a cash flowing property. That's what I call a win-win-win scenario, and I do those types of deals as much as I can! It's really hard to describe in words, but it's all good on paper.

The deals that you're involved in and the people that are educated and understand what they're doing provide so many opportunities for people to win.

Do you charge anything or do people have to be a client of yours to get the education you provide on self-directed IRA, both for people that want to open one, as well as people that want to work with these folks as lenders?

H. Quincy Long: No. We provide tons of free education to clients and potential clients alike. In my experience, when we have our classes, about half of the class are real estate investors who are looking for funding, or just looking to do networking. The other half of the class are clients of Quest IRA who are getting educated about how they can invest their IRAs. And by the way, I want to mention that lot of the people who do borrow money from Quest IRA clients are clients themselves. So clients do business with other clients.

The best way to be a self-directed IRA borrower is to be a self-directed IRA lender, because then you understand both sides of the deal. We have many clients that do business with each other.

That's a huge opportunity in itself.

What is one of the biggest and most common mistakes that people make when they're looking for a lender, especially at your networking events?

H. Quincy Long: Well, the biggest mistake that people make is that they don't know how to network. They don't know how to present themselves as an experienced investor.

The people who do networking the right way always have business cards with them for their real estate business. I can't believe how many people come to a networking session and have no business cards and no other information about what they do.

I always tell people to 'say it loud and say it proud' if you're a real estate entrepreneur. People need to be able to quickly identify what you do for a living. I like it when I see investors wear a bright shirt or something saying "I Buy Real Estate" to indicate what it is that they do. In addition to business cards and maybe a shirt with appropriate advertising, you always need to have your elevator speech ready.

In other words, if you're taking a ride in an elevator and somebody asks you what you do and you have one minute or less to educate them on what you do, you need to be able to communicate that clearly and effectively.

Another thing that I see people making a mistake about is not having what I call a "success book." Getting that first deal done is always the toughest. What I recommend people do is create a success book on every deal they do. This means they take a picture of the house in its worst state when they're buying it. They take pictures as the repairs are done. They take pictures when the rehab is completed and the house is looking fine. They take pictures of the settlement statement when they bought it, so it's clear what they paid for it. They include a list of the repairs that they did and a copy of that big fat check or wire that they get when they're done. That's what I call a success book. This is very impressive to potential lenders because it shows how serious you are as an investor.

It amazes me that people don't do that. If I was a full-time investor, that's exactly what I'd do because you want potential lenders to understand that you're serious about what you're doing and that you know what you're doing. It is a little tough to get that first one done, but if you get past that one, then you can succeed pretty well.

Basically it's all about effective networking. You need to be able to state your qualifications and speak confidently about your plans. You need to have all the answers to the questions that are typically or should be asked by potential lenders.

The people that are looking to invest their savings and their IRAs, are investing in people before they're investing in deals.

How often do you see people that are looking for money make the mistake of focusing primarily on, "I have this deal and I've got to close it by next Wednesday or I'm going to lose it." Instead of focusing on "Invest in me. I'm a success at what I do. The deal is incidental. I make successful deals."?

H. Quincy Long: That's exactly what I was trying to say. Private money lending is all about the relationship between you and the private money lender. Whatever you can do to convince people that you treasure that relationship above all else, that's going to get you more money than any particular deal will.

Now, of course, you have to still answer all the questions about the deal that you want to do, but the most successful private money borrowers from self-directed IRAs are actually those who sell themselves and then say, "Yeah, and by the way I've got some deals if you're interested in them." But basically, they sell themselves and convince people that they are reliable and knowledgeable investors in real estate.

Now let's talk about the people that have money.

If someone is interested in investing in real estate and they have some money in a retirement plan, can they use this money to fund the deals, rather than begging the banks and hard money lenders to do deals?

H. Quincy Long: Absolutely. Of course, the first thing to remember about investing your own IRA is that it's for your retirement. It's an Individual Retirement Account, not an Individual Right Now Account.

So you do have to remember that the investments you make in your IRA are for your future. Whereas, the investment you make with other people's IRAs loaning money to you are for your current needs. Self-directed IRAs apply both ways.

But you can buy real estate and you don't even need to have a whole lot of money to buy real estate if you're creative in the way that you do it.

Probably the biggest problem with self-directed IRAs is analysis paralysis. Going back to what I said earlier, these accounts are self-directed, and you do have to make your own decisions about how to invest your account. This means that to succeed you have to take the time to educate yourself on how to be a real estate investor and do what's necessary to establish the networks to achieve your goals.

That's a very important point. Your IRA is for your future, but perhaps another person's IRA is for your present.

How much money do you need? A lot of people think to invest in real estate or to loan money you need tens and tens of thousands of dollars. But, you've actually seen people start an IRA with as little as a few thousand dollars and grow it quickly.

There are people reading this book who may be wholesaling and may not have a lot of money. But there are actually people that have wholesaled properties out of their IRAs to grow that fairly quickly.

Can you give us one of those examples?

H. Quincy Long: That's true. There are a number of ways that you can use even a relatively small amount of money to invest in real estate.

One of the ways to invest with a small amount of money is wholesaling. Simply get a property under contract in your IRA and then assign that contract to another investor for a fee. However, you don't want to do a whole lot of that in your IRA because you're allowed to make investments in an IRA, not provide your services for free to your self-directed IRA. The old adage applies here: "Piglets get fed, but hogs get slaughtered."

You have to understand that it's all about making great investments. When clients buy an option on real estate in their IRA, that is an investment. An option is a right to buy property and, of course, that has value to it if you negotiate the right option.

I've seen people buy an option on real estate for $100 and turn around and sell that option to another investor for several thousand dollars. That happens on a fairly regular basis.

But wholesaling and options are not the only ways you can invest a relatively small amount of money. You can also bring in money partners on the investments.

For example, if you think about it, in the note example I gave earlier, that investor in Indiana is bringing me on as a money partner. He has very little or nothing in that deal, except for his knowledge and experience on investments.

If he wanted to do this in his IRA, he could get the property under contract in his IRA and bring me in as a money partner to fund most or all of the money needed for the deal. So that's another way to do it.

Another thing that you can do is buy property that is subject to debt. Now, that's getting a little bit advanced, but you can buy property subject to an existing loan, where the owner wants to walk away. Or you can even get private financing.

Your IRA can actually borrow money, subject to some restrictions, to buy an investment property. Those are all ways that people who don't have a whole lot of money but have a lot of good ideas can invest in real estate through their self-directed IRAs.

Some people may that think when you say IRA, you mean the Roth IRA. That it's the more flexible IRA that you can use for this type of stuff. But that's not the case, is it?

H. Quincy Long: No. That's just one of seven different types of accounts that can be self-directed and therefore can do all this fun stuff in real estate.

Accounts that you can self-direct include traditional IRAs, Roth IRAs, SEP IRAs, Simple IRAs, and even individual 401k plans, if you're self-employed and have no common law employees. Believe it or not, even Coverdell Education Savings Accounts for the kids' college education, or even high school education, and Health Savings Accounts can also be self-directed. I've had each and every one of those types of accounts at one time or another in my career, with the exception of the Simple IRA.

It's remarkable that people don't realize that. To be able to use even the college funding CESA is tremendous.

As a true educator and advocate, you always say there are different ways you can do this, but you don't promote doing this in an LLC so you can write checks out of that LLC.

H. Quincy Long: The LLC is a vehicle that some people should use in certain circumstances. It is certainly is not required to make investments in your IRA. It's actually is a bad idea to try to gain checkbook control of your IRA funds by the use of a Limited Liability Company.

People do invest in real estate notes and a whole lot of other stuff directly in their IRAs. Some people will use, as a justification, "I don't want to fill out all those forms" or "I don't want to pay those fees."

But they don't realize that it's good to have someone looking over your shoulder sometimes. Although we can't give tax, legal or investment advice, sometimes we can detect if people are not doing the right thing and prevent them from making a serious mistake.

Whereas, once you get it into an LLC, you have nobody looking over your shoulder, which you might think is a great idea. But, in fact, the rules can be kind of complex and it dramatically increases the possibility of actually doing a prohibited transaction by trying to gain checkbook control of your IRA.

By the way, if the government wanted you to have checkbook control of your IRA funds, they wouldn't require that a custodian or trustee have control of your funds. So I think that's a potential problem.

The fact that people don't really know the prohibited transaction rules is a also a big potential problem. The fact is these "checkbook control" IRA owned LLCs are often promoted by people that are basically just trying to sell you an expensive and often times unnecessary LLC. At Quest IRA, since we don't sell any investments or provide any tax, legal or investment advice, we can be completely neutral in saying these are the various ways that you can make investments in your IRA. We don't actually sell you on one particular way to structure your investments. An LLC is just another arrow in your quiver.

But it's not the only way to do it. At Quest IRA we don't actually allow our clients to have checkbook control over their IRAs by having themselves appointed as the manager of the LLC, although we will fund an LLC where another non-disqualified person is the manager.

That's probably one of those subtleties and advantages where you prevent people from doing things that fall outside the line and can get them into trouble.

Fear of the unknown is one of the biggest issues, especially in real estate investing. The fact that people are able to tackle that obstacle of the unknown without spending thousands of dollars on seminars to learn loopholes and tactics that may or may not be in their best interest is tremendous. And they don't have to be a client of yours to participate.

You talked a little bit about how you had your own IRA and you started networking with other people that had an IRA. What led you to decide there's a real need for this and to create this business?

H. Quincy Long: As I said, I did have a self-directed IRA, so I already understood the power of the self-directed IRA.

But when I first had the idea of starting Quest IRA, there wasn't a whole lot of education out there. And much of the education that was out there was frankly just wrong.

At first, I thought, "Wow, that's really cool that you can do all this stuff." But, you know, I am a lawyer. So I started studying the rules and I realized that what was being sold to people was just flat out wrong. Things like prohibited transactions were not really discussed. There's still a lot of that today, although I hope I've had some influence on the industry.

One of the things that I'm most proud about actually is that I have helped to educate people on the circumstances when their IRA investments may cause their IRAs to owe taxes. There are three circumstances in which an IRA, which normally pays no taxes on its gains, actually owes taxes on its profits. Not the IRA owner, but the IRA itself. These include owning a business in the IRA, renting personal property owned by the IRA, and owning debt-financed property in an IRA, either directly or indirectly.

That was a dirty little secret that was swept under the rug and hidden in the fine print of the account agreement. I got into the industry and I said, "We can't not disclose this. Because some of the things people are buying in self-directed IRAs have tax implications for the IRAs."

So me and another friend of mine who is a CPA just started educating clients about it. Now, it's a fairly commonly discussed issue called Unrelated Business Income Tax.

Basically, I started Quest IRA because I wanted to help people change their lives and their financial futures by freeing their IRAs up to invest in non-traditional investments like real estate. At the same time, I wanted to make sure that our clients received the tools and education necessary to build their retirement wealth while following the rules.

Having a passion to share this with others and help them has certainly made you one of the most respected and revered people in Houston real estate investing.

How can people find out more about Quest IRA and what the opportunities are there?

H. Quincy Long: Well, of course, we have our website at http://www.QuestIRA.com. You can also reach me by email at Quincy.Long@QuestIRA.com. Also, one of my favorite things is my blog. If you go to www.IRAWebAdvisor.com, there's a way to submit a question to me about self-directed IRAs. I actually read and answer those questions myself. If it's an interesting question, I'll post a sanitized version of the question and answer up on the blog.

There's a lot of information on the blog that's very interesting. Those are real questions asked by real people. My blog is a way to get not only an education, but get your questions answered.

About H. Quincy Long

H. Quincy Long is the President and founder of Quest IRA, Inc., and works in the Houston corporate office. Quincy has been a licensed Texas attorney since 1991, specializing in real estate, and has been a fee attorney for American Title Company. In 1990, Quincy received his Doctor of Jurisprudence degree from the University of Houston, and continued his education, receiving his Master of Laws degree in 1997. He has sat on the board of directors of the Realty Investment Club of Houston (RICH), the second largest real estate club in the country, and maintains the title of Certified IRA Services Professional, or CISP. Quincy is also the author of numerous articles on self-directed IRAs and other real estate related topics, many of which can be found on the Quest IRA website. In addition, Dyches Boddiford and George Yeiter, CPA, co-authored with Quincy to write the book "*Real Estate Investment Using Self-Directed IRAs and Other Retirement Plans.*" Widely known for his enthusiasm, attention to detail and knowledge of the Self-Directed retirement industry, he is one of the most sought after keynote speakers in the nation. Quincy can often be spotted in his office reading and learning more to prepare for one his many, highly-attended lectures on topics including self-directed retirement plans, real estate, unrelated business income tax, land trusts, mortgage foreclosures, etc. Quincy enjoys reading, hiking and spending time with family and friends in his free time.

Business Name:	Quest IRA, Inc.
Website:	www.QuestIRA.com
Facebook:	Facebook.com/QuestIRA
LinkedIn:	LinkedIn.com/Company/2413578
Twitter:	Twitter.com/QuestIRAInc
YouTube:	YouTube.com/User/QuestIRA

INVESTMENT REALTOR

David Lee Durr is a real estate agent who specializes in working with real estate investors as an expert consultant.

In this interview, David discusses the difference between the buy-and-hold strategy and the flipping or wholesaling strategy. In his opinion, someone who flips properties is a real estate "professional," like an agent, but should not be called an "investor," as they are mostly trading time for dollars vs. true investing where it is your money that is doing most of the hard work for you.

David's primary focus is helping his clients determine how to best utilize Real Estate as a tool to fund and free up their time to pursue their true life goals and passions. Those who work with David will learn primarily about the power of collecting "buy and hold" rental assets in order to build passive streams of income that send you checks each and every month, even long after the decision to stop actively pursuing new deals. He advocates using flipping as a tool to replenish seed money and for rapid expansion after developing a baseline familiarity with the skill-sets of property acquisition, renovation, and tenant management.

His experience and expert knowledge are evidenced from the first conversation with a client and partly shared in this chapter. He is truly an asset to both the experienced investor looking for the rare "investor-friendly agent" and those just starting out that think they may want to jump into the very lucrative real estate industry.

Conversation with David Lee Durr

You were a real estate investor before you became a real estate agent. Let's talk about that.

David Lee Durr: Yes, and I've since coined the phrase "Investment Realtor," to try and describe myself, which might actually sound like an oxymoron to many in the industry, because interestingly enough, most Realtors do not understand nor have a very fond opinion of Investors, and usually the feeling can be mutual.

You have to understand the way a majority of Realtors are trained is not designed to cater to investment real estate at all. That's a specialized niche well outside your typical "retail" (owner occupant) market that most agents do not even begin to understand, unless he/she is an investor him/herself. That's actually how I got into being a real estate agent – I was an already an investor, and I specifically became licensed to supplement my own investing.

Having more direct access to deals as an agent and already knowing exactly what I was looking for, I quickly realized it was not difficult to locate many more new deals each month than any single person could ever dream of taking on alone; therefore, I decided it made sense to share my knowledge as I passed along those opportunities to other investors in my area. The skill-set required to be an investor agent streamlined well with what I was already doing, and the extra revenue channel allows me to build my own portfolio even more aggressively...

...But the main thing for me really was being able to share my knowledge and strategies with others about the specifics of working investment real estate transactions -- something I tend to get *very* excited about.

On the other hand, most traditional real estate agents are retail-oriented. First of all, they get much higher commissions on a typical owner-occupant/retail sale than they would in the price range most investment deals makes sense at, which is no small motivation for someone living from one commission to the next, who is not an investor and does not have any passive income investments of their own.

Typical retail agent training consists mostly of how to find people looking to buy or sell, and then teach agents how to sell themselves as being "the best" at helping someone find their dream home or sell the one they have "faster" and at the "highest price" possible.

I will give you an insider tip though; however, it is not likely to make me very popular among some of my agent-peers: most retail houses sell on the MLS, and other than professional photography and staging there is very little in the way of "secret marketing strategies" that are likely to influence the price you net by a significant margin. For example, agents know open houses are very rarely the reason a house ends up selling to a specific buyer; the main reason agents do them -- it's a chance to find more potential clients.

To be fair, your agent's personality, experience, and communication skills may make a small difference during the negotiation phase and will definitely impact how educated and confident you feel throughout the process, but the main thing that determines the buyer's price is going to be the property itself.

So while many Realtors are busy working on how to better sell themselves, I'm spending most of my work-time focused on actually helping *educate* investors on finding, analyzing, properly rehabbing, and managing cash-flowing investment properties.

Oh, and another "fun" thing about typical investment deals is that they almost always come from the more difficult transaction sources such as foreclosures, short sales, distressed properties/homeowners, wholesalers, or other investors.

An example of an investor sale I might help facilitate is when an existing investor has built up equity over time and wants to take a group of their current tenant-occupied properties and sell them with the goal of 1031-exchanging the proceeds into a small multi-family apartment deal or maybe a bigger package of single-family houses.

A lot of extra headaches come with selling these types of properties. For example, dealing with the banks or government on foreclosures and short sales or coordinating inspections, rehab bids, appraisals, and surveys on a tenant-occupied home. Many agents, (and even some investors), will not touch a certain type of transaction. They will say things like, "I won't even look at a short sale" or "I don't show or bid on auction properties."

In addition to the inherit extra difficulty of these deals, investors are also much more willing to walk away from a deal than someone in love with their dream home. So a very large percent of the showings and contracts written will never materialize into actual closings, especially short-sales and auction based foreclosures. This makes most agents feel they are wasting their time, and that can be deadly in a commission based profession.

...And even if the transaction *does* go through, it is always at least twice as much work jumping through bank and government hoops and problem solving for a much smaller commission in the end, since payoff is calculated by property price, not work involved, and investment properties are the cheapest properties being sold.

One of the biggest differences I am allowed in my business approach is that I personally don't depend on commissions from my Realtor transactions. I make a lot more on just one of my own investments, especially my long term hold properties, than I do on the commissions from doing 10 deals for other people, …

...But I absolutely love being involved with and teaching other people, and since I already have more than enough passive income from my own rentals to cover my bills even if I stop working altogether, I can focus on what I love doing vs. what I "need" to do.

There have actually been multiple times where I decided to take a break for a full month or two because of family emergency, traveling, or different things that come up. My main point though is: because I'm not caught up in the typical feast/famine cycle most Realtors find themselves in, it allows me to run my business from a completely different set of priorities.

I am actively practicing what I preach by not being tied down financially and pursuing my passions. My Realtor activities are just a manifestation of one of those passions, which is teaching and sharing something of true value with others, especially about the system and tools that freed me up in the first place. Since I've experienced first-hand the power and impact of real estate investing, I'm very passionate about educating my consumers and giving them the information they need to make real estate work for them too...

...But there are caveats they need to understand going in. First, it is going to require a lot of hard-work on the front-end. Second, they need to go out and actually do it themselves, (no one else is actually going to pull the trigger for you), and justifying procrastination is not going to get it done either, And finally, no matter how awesome you are, it will not be an overnight process, (which is all the more reason to get started sooner rather than later).

I want them to escape the instinctual lure of short-term instant gratification and understand the very real and powerful effects of an effective strategy compounding on itself over the long-term.

You brought up some very important points.

Most real estate agents are transaction based and that's how they make their money. You seem much more relationship based, which seems like a huge benefit to your clients.

Talk about your first meeting with someone that's interested in working with you to purchase real estate.

David Lee Durr: To be fair, I am transaction based in one sense, but thankfully, it's not from the need to figure out how much food I can put on the table this month. However, I use transaction numbers as an indicator of how big of an impact I am making in the community and on the people I am working with.

On the one hand, it is not difficult to find someone who is "interested" in real estate investing. Almost everybody out there knows on some level that it is a very lucrative opportunity and is interested in "learning more" or "getting into it at some point," but anyone who has been around investment clubs a while can also attest that it is more common to run into a seminar and information junkies who would rather talk, attend meetings, read books, look at YouTube videos (or even worse: HGTV) or read blogs all day...than someone willing to actually go out, get over their fears, and put in the work required to make transactions happen.

Unfortunately, I personally have some resources that are always going to be limited. I only have so much time and energy to spend with people, (a good portion of which is already set aside for my family), and given the depth of knowledge that I enjoy giving to those I work with, I need to have some accountability to make sure I am not robbing resources from people willing to work and wasting it on tire kickers. I use transaction numbers to make sure I am actually being productive in my consultation activities.

I have to take some of the limits of my own personality into account. I don't like to turn anyone away, and usually, whoever I am with, I like to give them my full focused attention during the time we share. I try to answer questions as fully as possible, to the point that sometimes I have to stop and make sure I am not rambling or "over-educating" beyond their interest or need to make a confident decision.

If I notice their eyes start to glaze over, then I have probably already gone too far and I'm no longer being effective. The problem is, I'm usually so focused, I don't notice that look; (at least that's what my wife tells me).

...And when it comes to e-mails, I'm not much better. I've had colleagues pick on me at times for writing "mini-novels" due to my tendency to want to be very thorough and clear in my communications, (especially anything in writing).

However, if I am going to be investing a significant amount of time, energy and thought consulting and advising someone, I prefer to know who is going to take what I am offering and turn it into something of value through a decision to actually take action.

Therefore, I also try to make a point at the end of each discussion to layout the next expectation and time frame. There is nothing wrong with philosophical discussion, but my purpose in this is to make an impact and a real world difference, so in addition to education and information I also need to make sure everyone stays action-oriented on moving forward.

For example, phrases I often say are things like: "When I get back to a computer tonight, I can run an evaluation and send it to you to review" or (after walking a property): "my wife will work on drawing up the docs now so you can digi-sign, and we can send in the offer by tonight," "I've sent the offer, I will follow-up with them daily and let you know as soon as I have a response," or "Hey, they just let me know our offer was accepted; I need to meet with you today or tomorrow for the option and earnest money checks."

If we don't meet a specific goal post, I understand life doesn't always go as planned, so I'll follow-up to see what happened: "Hey, what's going on? I didn't get the documents back from you yet. Did it go through?" I need to know if it's a technology error, the human component of just being busy, or fears of second-thoughts creeping in or unanswered questions, so I know what to do next.

If it becomes a habit that I notice someone consistently not moving forward, then unfortunately, not from my choice, but from their own, I allow them to make the decision to stay in their comfort zone and current situation while I spend my time with the next person who is going taking action and moving forward on what they said they would do.

However, at the same time, I also have to be able to reign in the "jump first, ask questions later" guys from just running around from one bright shiny idea to another.

In the initial stages of my consultations, I try to lay out clear expectations of what exactly that investor is trying to achieve and of how much time, energy, and effort can reasonably be expected to pursue that.

"Let's look at your overall big picture goals and strategize the most effective use of your resources. Let's go over all your questions and concerns. Let's go over the expectations and time-line of a full transaction. Let's NOT just take action for action's-sake, spray and pray, putting in offer after offer until one gets accepted, and *then* think about what comes next, which is going to lead to later looking back and saying "I wish I had/hadn't done _____.' "

For example, I have had investors put out so many offers at once that were simultaneously accepted, lending guidelines required they put down 25% of purchase price on ALL of the properties under contract, but if they had just waited on one of them, they could have stayed within the loan limits to only put down 20% on those 3-4 deals, before moving into the next tier of higher down payment requirements. This scenario is just one of the things I try to help them identify *before* we create the issue, rather than having to make tough decisions after the fact.

In the beginning stages, I am sitting down and looking at their specific situation, stated goals, and resources. Then I am strategically applying years of research and experience to formulate advice on what I think would be an effective, efficient path to putting those resources to work towards those goals. I get a few people that will listen, and they are the ones that keep me excited and motivated, but I have also had to come to terms with accepting that Pareto's Principle (the 80/20 rule) is very much in effect when it comes to those willing to accept someone else's (even a professional's) advice on *their* financial decisions.

So, I learned to stop taking it personally for the 80% who are insistent on inaction, or doing it their own way, or for example, the ones who are not comfortable doing *anything* until they know everything there is to know about a particular subject. The problem they run into is that Real Estate Investing requires specialized knowledge from so many different fields from legal and tax consequences, understanding different layers of insurance, to engineering and construction components covering everything from electrical, plumbing, roofing, foundation, HVAC, pest control, managing contractors, then marketing for, qualifying, and managing tenants, etc. etc. (to infinity and beyond).

So the person that's looking to be an absolute expert in every one of these fields will have no shortage of new material to study. They could easily find enough content to continue studying and coming up with new questions to their hearts content for at least 70 years or so, and to be honest, that is exactly what a lot of people would prefer to do, rather than go out there and actually make a decision at risk that it might not be the absolute "best" or optimal one they "could" have made. I try to remind people they don't need to know *everything,* they just need to know *enough,* enough to be effective. It is easy to forget those aren't the same thing.

Also, too often, people do not understand the opportunity costs. For example, the 80% extra time it might take to become an expert in a field vs. the person willing to simply go out there and take the 20% needed to consistently make rapid-fire *productive* decisions. The most successful individuals, as measured by the ones achieving the most *results*, tend to be those who opt to build teams of professionals they can trust to be experts in the 80% and give them the 20% needed to keep moving forward.

Another benefit of relying on experts, besides the obvious leveraging of their knowledge, is just the fact that they are usually a lot more efficient at their specific tasks and skills, since they are using them every day vs. an equally competent person trying to run every single component of their own deal from start to finish.

There are several very real reasons systems like assembly lines and global trade increase overall net productivity as much as they do, (one of which is again related to opportunity cost and how the exact same task can actually "cost" one person *more* than another who is equally qualified and has the exact same time and money requirements, but may be sacrificing different "opportunities" available to them in order to complete the task).

What I am trying to do with my clients is leverage my knowledge and strategic mindset to help minimize opportunity costs and maximize results reflecting steps towards their specific end-goals and passions. I try to keep the big picture in mind and remind them throughout, that it's generally not just about making X number of dollars or eventually only having to work Y number of hours per month, but it is about using Real Estate as a tool to put X and Y together in a balanced equation that eventually results in a life reflective of what you truly love, care about, and want to spend your time and money on in this world.

Unfortunately, the vast majority of people are not (and will never) live a life based on what they truly love and is important to them at the deepest level, but instead will live it mostly based on what they "must do" as dictated by someone else. This is probably going to sound cheesy, but that is extremely saddening to me, and I feel extremely lucky to have personally found the opportunities in real estate that I did.

I know that ultimately I won't be able to save the world, but I feel driven to make what difference I can with the opportunities I have, and right now, kind of ironically, that means helping others understand and assess what opportunities they have and what they may be passing over without even realizing or thinking about it.

In the end, I am not specifically an advocate of Real Estate for its own sake for any other reason except that it is the most effective (and accessible) tool I have found in being able to free people to have both the time and money needed to live a life of meaning and purpose to them and not simply out of survival or "necessity".

That is, if they will listen, when I try to explain things like the difference between true investing in long-term buy and hold rentals which results in both an *ever-increasing* and *increasingly passive* income, as opposed to just flipping or wholesaling, which can undoubtedly create revenue, (assuming you do it right), but you are still always going to be limited to trading time for that money, which in the end, is not much different from many of the millions of other non-real estate jobs out there to choose from.

The goal is to help people realize, you really can use real estate as a tool to build_passive income, and free up your time to pursue whatever your true life passions are. I hope to let investors understand the reality of their dreams being achievable and hopefully to eventually expand those dreams even bigger, but to also accept reasonable expectations of what it takes to get there. It is absolutely not going to happen overnight, nor is it going to happen without putting in the necessary time, energy, effort, and money required, Investing requires by definition, that you put something in to get something out.

However, if you are willing to practice the discipline of delayed gratification, front load the work, and start putting your resources to work for you, instead of consuming everything immediately, then patiently, over time, the magic of compounding growth can go to work for you, and eventually, even replace you as the primary worker, altogether.

There's a saying that's very true: "most people overestimate what they can do in one year and underestimate what they can do in five." It is even more true when you're dealing with something that has a compounding effect and exponential growth potential like real estate.

So I have to learn how to try and balance both people resistant to ever doing anything, and those addicted to instant gratification, that will do anything at first, but if it's not fast enough, they are likely to flake out and run around looking for another new, "faster," shiny, bright idea before giving their Real Estate the time it needs to mature into a self-sustaining monster.

It's not uncommon for people to come to me having calculated their idea of the number of houses they need to replace their current income, and then say "my goal is to buy ___ houses within the next twelve months and then maybe move into multi-family."

Unfortunately, most of them are also coming in with a very inaccurate idea of the actual time and energy it will require to go through that many transactions and solve all the various problems that come up during the process, ...and problems always come up. That is part of what we are getting paid for, to take on that risk and figure out how to solve them If it were as easy as everyone's idealized fantasy land tries to make it out to be, there would be a lot more people actually out there doing it.

In reality, I do know several established investors who routinely buy 50-100 houses a year, and even a few who have bought that many during their first 2-3 years in the business, but that is the aggressive side of the industry (and sometimes your competition). It is definitely the exception and not the rule for a rookie to enter any new industry, and in their first year join the top 1% who have years of momentum behind them.

However, almost anyone can take where they are at now, and pending where their personal situation, if needed take a couple of years to get out of debt, fix credit issues, and save up some money, preferably while they learn and develop a foundation of knowledge at the same time. Then plan to pick up just one or two houses their 1st year buying, then buy two or three their 2nd year.

If they stay disciplined, (which is the fatal "if" for most), and instead of spending their extra cash-flow on an ever-increasing lifestyle immediately, use the art of delayed gratification, add it to their continued savings for down payments on future properties, then each year they will be able to pick up more properties faster.

So their 3rd year, they may still be taking it easy and only buy three to five more, but by years four and five, they could easily pick up five to ten each year, because they have both a much more solid base financially than when they were first starting, and they have had time and experience to fine tune both their skill sets and set realistic expectations.

With current deal cash flows of $400-$500/mo each house, that plan would up eventually resulting in between $6,400/mo (1+2+3+5+5 houses*$400) on the low end and $15,000 (2+3+5+10+10 houses *$500) on the more aggressive side. Most people can afford to not "have to" work anymore at those income levels, but if not, they now have a skill-set to design whatever lifestyle they can imagine in a relatively short period of time.

Five to even seven years sounds like forever at first, (especially compared to all the garbage, unrealistic, something for nothing, get rich quick programs out there preying on people's nature to feed their instant gratification monkeys,) but compared to the "traditional" track of spending four to twelve years getting a degree, and then working twenty, thirty, or forty years, just to "retire", (usually at poverty income level by the way, but that is a whole other discussion), the seven year plan doesn't look so bad.

The Flip This House TV shows make people think flipping is the way to build wealth. You believe both flipping and a buy-and-hold strategy should be part of a long-term investment plan.

When should someone focus on flipping a property versus doing long-term hold?

David Lee Durr: Yes, did I mention I'm kind of a fan of the buy and hold philosophy? I am also surrounded by many very successful investors, who not only share my ideas, but live the results of the wealth it affords. However, when I am talking about real estate investing with the average person off the street, they often start referring to flipping houses, which makes me have to stop for a second and remember: this person's idea of "real estate investing" is probably coming from HGTV or show with the name "flip" in the title claiming to be about "investing."

In the circles I travel, there is a chance you might get scorned if you refer to the "F-word" as investing, because by definition, investing money is putting your *money* to work for you, but when you're flipping, you're very much out there *working* for your money – which is the 180 degree opposite reality of our goal, because if you stop working, the money will stop coming in also.

Don't get me wrong, there is definitely work involved in buying a rental asset. However, the vast majority of that work, when done correctly, is front-loaded during the acquisition phase. Once the property is stabilized, you can choose to be either "semi-passive" and manage the property yourself, or truly passive and pay someone else to do it, but either way, the money still keeps coming in.

That is assuming you follow best practice and do things correctly, some of which can seem a bit counter-intuitive to at first, but are tried and true principles that successful investors have been following for years.

For example, a lot of rookies getting in falsely believe the road to a bigger bottom line lies somewhere in taking the "cheap" way out of things, maybe on property repairs or upgrades, maybe in negotiations, etc.

Now you definitely do not want to go out with the plan to sink as much money as possible into making all of your rental properties as "pretty" as your own personal home, (which is actually the opposite, but still very common mistake to "over-rehab"), but you also do not want to always try to skate by on the "cheapest" solutions.

In the long run, cheap can often end up costing you more time, energy, money, phone calls, and hassle than if you had just spent the correct amount of money to have it done right. The goal is to create clean, safe, functional, living space and provide it to families who can't afford, (or in the case of millennials, choose not to take on the responsibilities of) homeownership themselves, and for you to do so at a profit.

An easy example can be illustrated using flooring. Some people will automatically opt for as much carpet as possible, since it is the cheapest up-front. I personally prefer a flooring called vinyl-plank, which a lot of commercial buildings have been using for years, that only slightly more expensive on the front end, but because it is so much more durable and easier to maintain, after you factor in re-placement costs at tenant turnover, you save a ton of money in the long run. (Plus, personally I think it looks nicer).

A rule of thumb many investors use in deciding how to rehab a rental property is by expecting that you will be holding it for 3-5 years. The actual metric I use for deciding when to liquidate one of my rentals is based off of the opportunity cost of its current cash-flow vs. the total cash flow of reinvesting the net equity sitting in the prop-erty, but that is a discussion for another time...

...What were we talking about originally before my tangents? Oh yeah, people referring to flipping as "investing."

The thing is, you go out and you flip a house (and lets not discount that there is a very good chance you can do it wrong, especially on your first few deals), but even if you do it right, just know the TV standards of making a quick $30,000 or $50,000 check is not as com-mon or easy as they would like you to believe, especially for beginners.

Its also not uncommon for them to misrepresent the numbers they are giving in different ways. Often they will give projected, not real, numbers of what they *expect* to make, or there are all kinds of ways they try to fudge the numbers to hide things like true holding or clos-ing costs, or the biggest thing they usually fail to mention: the true tax consequences.

Of course everyone's tax situation is different, (which is a good ex-cuse to just ignore it on a TV show), but at least understand that whenever you flip a property in under twelve months, you not only have capital gains to consider, you are also considered self-employed according to the IRS (even they call it what it is, a form of employment - not investing) and you are liable to pay both employer and employee sides of social security, on top of your 25% cap gains hit. You're often paying over 40% and sometimes as much as 50% of your "profit," immediately payable to Uncle Sam's unless you want to find yourself in a bit of trouble come tax-season.

So that $30,000 becomes $15,000 real quick.

Now, if for example, you're living off of around $4,000 or $5,000 per month, it's not hard to see how you can expect to say goodbye to the remaining $15,000 in the next three months. In light of the the time factor of a typical transaction: You have to go find a deal, perform due diligence, go through closing, manage contractors to rehab, market the property for sale, and then wait for a buyer to put in an offer, inspect, negotiate, and finally, spend a month waiting for their loan to get approved through underwriting and close again. On a typical flip, you should expect at least anywhere from a 3-6 month timeline.

So that means as soon as you close on one deal, and while you are still managing it, you need to also be looking for your next one just so you can continue paying the bills and putting food on the table.

So again: that's not investing if you're just trading one job for another. That's being a real estate professional, and there is absolutely nothing wrong with that. There are a lot of great things about just being in the real estate industry, but lets call it what it is. You don't call a Realtor, loan officer, or contractor a "real estate investor" just because they make money in the field of real estate.

True investing is where you buy property which requires work and skill, but the goal is to put a tenant in there and a year later, you're still getting checks in the mail from the fruits of your labor done long ago.

Every year or two, you might have to go and re-show or renew a lease, but you're spending a couple of hours on maintenance, to keep those $400 or $500 checks flowing every month (or you could just hire a property manager and plan to buy a few more houses to pay for the additional "cost").

Unfortunately, to most, $400 or $500 forever doesn't sound like a lot compared to a $30,000 check now. That's why the instant gratification industry is built on programs selling fantasy $30,000 check now vs $400 or $500 a month, but $400 or $500 every month adds up to around $6,000 a year, ...and assuming you plan on living at least another 5 years, it is obviously the higher paying option.

Oh, and by the way, that is only *one* of the ways your money is hard at work for you in the long-term real estate game. You're also passively enjoying market appreciation, which a lot of investors refer to as the icing on the cake, because it's not something that we buy for, but it is a reality.

And bear in mind: while real estate markets do go up and down over the short term, in the long run, they always go up. Data has shown that in nearly any market a property will approximately double in price over a 20 year period.

So what should you reasonably expect in a stable market like Houston, where we don't have the rapidly violent up and down swings like they do in places such as California, Florida, or New York, but instead we have a generally consistent slow and steady growth?

Well there's a resource on HAR.com and NeighborhoodScout where you can look up the actual average appreciation in a market over the past six months, year, three years, five, ten, fifteen years, but I use 3% when I'm estimating appreciation, just because that's a generally acceptable yearly cost of living or inflation adjustment to expect. If you look at the stats, at least here in Houston, actual appreciation is significantly higher.

But, here's the cool thing: first I advocate proper leverage, which means for example, not paying 100k cash to only buy one house, renting it out for 1200, but after subtracting out 300/mo in taxes and insurance, only netting 900/mo for your 100k invested, (that's *only* a 10.8% return), when you could take that same 100k and instead buy 4-5 properties at 20-25k down each ending up with a total cash flow of $1600-$2500/mo, (making 19.2-30% just on cash flow).

And as a bonus, that 3% appreciation on the house value of 100k house, is a 3k gain on only 20k invested, which is much higher than a 3% return on appreciation.

It's about 15%.

David Lee Durr: So that's another 15% each year you are earning just by owning an inflation adjusted asset. By the way, both our rents and property values are protected and adjusted for inflation, which is not something a lot of other types of investments can claim.

But wait, there's more! On top of that, your tenant is paying down *your* mortgage debt for you. Of course, it's not going to be a lot in the beginning, because of the way the mortgage industry front loads interest, but since we calculate our cash flow returns *after* all the principal, taxes, insurance, interest, etc. that our tenant's rent is paying for us, it's a nice little bonus return that they are the ones paying the house down, but we are the ones who end up with the equity in the end.

Also, since markets do drop in the short term, if you're making $400 or $500 a month on a house, you don't need to sell it right now. Of course, if you're trying to flip the property short term and you timed things wrong, that is going to hurt. A lot of times, it will put a huge wave of flippers out of business all at once when the market starts to dip.

But, if you're buying a hold property and the market goes down, you can just wait for it to come back up. That's what history tells us it will do. It'll go down for a while, but ultimately, it will come back up, eventually, even higher than it was before.

But as a hypothetical, let's say for some reason the market somehow never recovers. You still can't lose, because there is going to be some point where that tenant has paid down your mortgage low enough that you would still be able to sell it, no matter what the new value is, and end up taking a check home. If you end up having to hold it for a full thirty years, then what happens? You are now the proud owner of a property free and clear of any mortgage debt... Thank you tenants.

And finally, when you're investing long term (the way even the IRS defines it), all of the sudden Uncle Sam is now in your corner vs. extorting you up for half of your "profit" every year.

Why? Well it probably has something to do with the saying that legislators write laws, not for citizens, but for themselves, ... and guess where a very large percentage of legislators (and the wealthy in general) tend to hold their wealth – in real estate of course.

So there are all kind of tax loopholes like straight-line and accelerated depreciation, doing deferments such as 1031 exchanges indefinitely until their estate gets a "step-up-in-basis," which effectively wipes out everything that was deferred, tapping into equity via cash-out refis, which are not taxed since they are debt, (but it is debt that your tenants end up paying off for you), etc. Now you are actually able to enjoy tax benefits vs. penalties from owning real estate long term.

As an example, there is a well-known investor here in Houston who literally puts many millions of dollars in his bank account each year, and yet still gets a six-figure tax refund from the IRS.....legally.

Bottom Line: If you want to build long-term wealth, it's going to be from the buy and hold strategy. That is what the system is built to incentivize, and it does so very well.

Flipping can still have its place of course, in my opinion you can use it as a tool to either maximizing your initial seed money, or maybe replenish it when you start to run low on big chunks of cash, preferably after you have a solid foundation in real estate already though.

Strategy will be dictated by all kinds of factors of course, such as where the investment money is coming from. Is it a renewable source, such as saving from a steady income while living below your means or is it from a one time event, such as an inheritance, selling a business, or some other windfall of money that you need to stretch before you start putting it to work at its steady job.

Personally, I prefer anyone looking to risk a large chunk of money on a flip already be comfortable with the real estate process by having bought three or four rental properties, because expectations are likely to be more realistic, and acquisition and rehab skill-sets are already sharper, helping mitigate some risks a brand new investor faces.

Also, I often find the people I work with rarely fall in love with the process of actually "doing" real estate. They like the passive income it provides, but not the day-to-day transactional problems you're dealing with on every deal.

Despite what a lot of gurus might have you believe, the truth is transactions are not what most people would define as "easy." Even most real estate agents have a very short lifespan in the industry, usually under 2-3 yrs. There are a lot of cookie-cutter tasks and formulas, but there are also a lot of details and work involved that can make or break you.

A lot of my clients have other things they would rather be doing than more deals, and sometimes it's actually their primary job. They know they need passive income long-term for retirement and legacy, but they don't want to do any more real estate more than they have to for their goals. They don't want to be constantly managing a bunch of flips full-time. They prefer to just go ahead and do a slow and steady pace of buying a couple of houses this year, take a break to recuperate, and then buy a couple more houses next year.

And if that makes them happy and meets their goals, then hey, they are building a nice supplemental or replacement income while they continue to work at a job they love, and there is nothing wrong with that at all.

Fear-based decisions come up, especially when people are first getting into real estate. It sounds like long-term, buy and hold can be more forgiving than doing flips if someone makes a mistake.

Talk about the common fears you see in your new clients and how they deal with them.

David Lee Durr: Long-term investing is absolutely more forgiving than trying to get rich quick, that I think I already hit on pretty hard.

But no matter what, for most people it's uncomfortable to write big checks, especially in the beginning when everything is so unfamiliar. Ultimately it is their decision to make and my role is just do my best to educate them and remind them of how our best practices work and keep us operating the same way the casinos do, where even if we lose a hand every once in a while, the system is built so the house always wins, (and we just want to own all the houses).

But in all seriousness, I have found myself operating as a part time psychologist dealing with human aspect and emotional side of things, as often as a consultant dealing with the human intellect on the more straightforward math, logic, and strategy involved. Luckily, I like to study psychology and neurology for fun, two more subject our study-bugs can add to their list along with things like negotiations, marketing, accounting...

(30 minutes later) ...Sorry, I get lost in my own tangents sometimes. What was the topic? Oh yeah, dealing with people's emotions. When my wife and I were at West Point, everything we did, from how big of bites we took to how we performed at any given task was put under a microscope and given back to us in reference to the leadership influence we were going to reflect on other people's decisions. So I like to dissect and think about what influences people to make all the choices they do and what makes the human mind work the way that it does.

In my experience, I have found though we like to try to fool ourselves into thinking otherwise, often it's not our logic or intellect that ends up making the decision as much as we think. Emotions are a much stronger motivator and dictator of action than logic. As a result, if someone has an emotional block, you can't argue their emotions away. It doesn't work. It's like trying to argue with an angry pit bull.

I generally try to listen to root of their fears, if possible, validate what is reasonable and understandable, and then I simply remind them of their options, and let them make whatever decision they are comfortable with.

What are some of those common fears that people have as they're making the decision to purchase a property?

David Lee Durr: I always advise my buyers to have a licensed inspector check the property during their due diligence period. One example of a sticking point is if the buyer is at all nervous or shaky, it will often bubble up when they get that inspection report.

Those reports can be long and seem scary sometimes. It has a purpose, which is to lay out every single *possible* thing that could be perceived as a flaw. For example, if a house was built a few decades ago, there have been a lot of changes in building codes that the property is grandfathered in on and not necessarily something you need to worry about too much from a functional or safety standpoint, (if it were they wouldn't allow grandfathering), but that the inspector is required to disclose on a report.

Because interpreting these reports can be tricky sometimes, I usually want my buyers to try to plan to speak to the inspector in person about it, preferably during the last 20 min. of the inspection when it is still fresh in his mind to help determine: “What in this report is a serious health, safety, or functionality concern?”

So my approach is to simply deal with the situation with information, by talking to the professional and relying on his expertise to allow the investor make an informed decision. I also try to constantly remind what are reasonable expectations and the overall goal.

For example, you will never find a 100% perfect flawless home, even in a brand new construction, but our job isn’t to have a perfect house. Our goal is to provide a home that’s clean, safe, and functional at market rents where we can own and operate the property at a profit to fund our desired quality of life.

Another sticking point that comes up is often worry over the projected value of a house. As a realtor, I give them my opinion of value based on the comparable sales in the area. But, my buyers aren't always convinced and that's perfectly fine.

Usually the official appraisal is one of the last things that is done in the process, almost always outside of the option or due diligence period. So they're worried that if the appraisal comes back lower than they're expecting, their out-of-pocket costs may be higher and they will not end up getting as good of a deal as they were initially expecting.

Well, again my approach is just to provide as much information as I can, and let them know what their options are, including talking to another expert, and let them make a decision. Especially, because worry over appraised value is actually a legitimate concern. It is a subjective sport, and often even two different appraisers will come up with significantly different values.

I talk with appraisers all the time, and I know some that boast about being intentionally conservative. They'll outright tell you the number they appraise at is at isn't necessarily same as what a realtor could sell it for today. Their main job is to keep their clients (which are the banks and the lenders) happy by keeping their exposure low.

During the due diligence period, I can also direct my buyers to three appraisers to choose from that I know will give them a better analysis than the straight price per square foot tool most Realtors use, which is a great starting point of value to help determine which deals are worth looking at further, but it definitely isn't as in depth as an appraisal.

So one option if they are really worried is they can pay about $99 to get a "desktop appraisal," which is the full appraisal process short of visiting the property in person, but using desktop public information instead, and it gives a much more accurate picture of what you should expect the full appraisal to come back at usually within a 2-3% margin of error, than a Realtor's evaluation.

...But again even appraisers disagree with one another on their opinions of value, and markets can change from one month to the next. It's a risk that you either learn to mitigate and be comfortable with or that you decide is enough to keep you from doing real estate at all.

So yes, over time, I am often dealing with many of the same sticking points in the process for people to get hung up on and stall at. I just stay focused on trying to find solutions, and help them make an informed decision, because in the end, it all just comes down to them deciding if this property's risk/reward ratio is tolerable for them.

Each person is has a different threshold for risk and your ability to work with that is one of the huge benefits to working with you.

How can people find out more about David Lee Durr and how to get involved if that's a step that they're ready to make?

David Lee Durr: I am currently in the process of rehabbing my website, which is www.LeeDurr.com, so it is under construction, but in the meantime, if they want to reach out to me by calling or texting, I have a business line connected to both mine and my wife's phone at 832-800-DURR (3877).

My wife and I work together as a team, each playing to our preferred strengths in the transaction process, so with us you get two experts for the price of one, and our synergy helps make it more like a 1+1=3 situation.

For example, many times I will walk a property with a client and while I'm driving home, she's already written the contract and sent it to their e-mail to be digitally signed, so we can get it submitted as soon as possible

Especially in a seller's market, like the one we have now, where deals are gone very quickly, you have to be able to enable your clients to make smarter, faster decisions, than the other guys so we can stay out in front as a Market Leader (or LeeDurr) making the biggest impact on our clients lives and the community as we can.

About David Lee Durr

Business Name: The Lee Durr Team

Website: LeeDurr.com

Facebook: Facebook.com/LeeDurrTeam

LinkedIn: LinkedIn.com/pub/David-LeeDurr/b7/6a0/a02

Twitter: @LeeDurrTeam

YouTube: YouTube.com/channel/UCcDGSU39f1bOOINzD2JaFZw

Pinterest: Pinterest.com/LeeDurrTeam

REAL ESTATE INVESTOR PROJECT ADVISOR

Chris Adkins works for Invest Home Pro as a project consultant and advisor. As a real estate investor himself, he knows the value of getting good advice on a project, as well as having a team behind him to help with the decisions and the work that go into a project.

In this interview, Chris discusses many of the pitfalls that new investors may encounter in evaluating a project. He also shares the best approach to take when rehabbing properties for flipping, versus for long-term renting.

Chris' focus is helping both new and seasoned real estate investors use the best approach and plan to ensure they are getting the highest return on investment for the proposed use for the property in question.

His many years of experience in this industry also enable him to help in an educational and consultative manner. Investors are the lucky beneficiaries of Chris Adkins' knowledge.

Conversation with Chris Adkins

One part of construction that people struggle with is their fear of not knowing how to fix a house or what needs to be done to a house to get it ready to sell.

What's the mindset of an investor and how do you recommend what changes will help bring the highest sales price?

Chris Adkins: This is the part that can make or break your investment. Obviously, it's pretty easy to figure out what you're buying a house for and when talking to a realtor or any real estate professional, you can figure out what you can sell the house for.

The part that everyone gets scared of is how much is construction going to cost and what needs to be done. In our coaching, we make things pretty simple, cut and dried. We just measure the market by looking at comparable sales. We see what was done to the houses, as far as work goes. Then we try to mimic those changes as closely as possible.

We believe that if we can bring a house up to the same condition as the other houses in the same neighborhood that have sold for top dollar, then that house should also sell for top dollar.

A lot of people look to you as a trusted advisor.

Infomercials and investment packages imply that it takes a special intuition to determine the best investment. The fact is you go by the numbers and you go by the evidence of the neighborhood.

Would you say that a neighborhood may not be the best place to invest if there's not enough data?

Chris Adkins: Yes. There are very few markets like that in and around Houston, but you're absolutely right. There is this myth propagated by HGTV and all these fixing house shows that you're going to need a special high-end designer or some European influence, architecture or something like that. The reality is that by just analyzing the market in and around you, you can see what people are looking for and what they're paying the most for.

You lose some of those comparables in some of the rural markets on the fringes of Houston. But you can always widen your search area and maybe instead of just looking in that neighborhood, you look at neighborhoods around it. Eventually, you're going to find something comparable.

A lot of people want to jump right in and make it a palace so it'll sell. Oftentimes, that can dip into the profit.

How important is it to see what the other houses that are selling in that market look like and what level of updating and customization they have?

Chris Adkins: I'd say that's one of the most important things you need to look at on the way in to a deal. Just for the pure fact that that's how you're going to find out what the actual value of the house is going to be after it's repaired. Then, obviously, that's how you're going to find out what you need to do.

One of the big dangers we see a lot of new investors getting into is either they want to significantly over-rehab it or they want to just barely do anything to it and then somehow increase the prices tens of thousands of dollars and make all this money.

When you analyze that and you look at it, there is a diminishing law of return on what you're putting into the house versus the dollars you're going to get out of it.

A wise friend of mine once told me about the minimum effective dose theory. He said you can spend all this time and effort doing it perfectly and doing it to the nines. Or you can make it very similar to all the other houses in the neighborhood that have sold for the right price and not spend a lot of time over-rehabbing it and you'll get that perfect return on your investment for what you're putting into it.

Well, that's certainly a skill in itself to try to identify that.

When you describe what you do, not as a remodeler and not in construction, you work specifically with real estate investors, correct?

Chris Adkins: Yes. I can't say we only do investment properties, because we have done one or two owner-occupied properties, but that is very few and far between. For the most part, 99% of our business comes from investors either looking to rehab to sell as a flip, or rehab to rent as a long-term investment. That's really what we focus on.

When you initially started talking about swinging hammers and laying tile – to be honest with you, I don't know how to do a whole lot of that myself. I know how to manage it and get it done for the right price and do it effectively. But I'm not necessarily a construction specialist so much as we are an investment company that does contracting.

You manage construction and remodeling projects specifically as investments.

There are a lot of moving parts to managing a project and most people wonder if they can come in under their financial budget, but there's also a budget of time involved.

Talk about the variables of time and finance that can affect the bottom line of an investment project.

Chris Adkins: Many entrepreneurs want to run million dollar companies and have their time be valuable, but then you find them in the office doing $10 an hour tasks. We take away all the micromanaging and all the $10 an hour tasks.

We boil it down to; if you just give us the keys to your house, we'll give you a budget, a timeline. And you can come back whenever that timeline's complete and we'll give your keys back and you'll have a rehabbed house.

A lot of newbie investors try to manage projects themselves and end up putting way too much time into the project. They end up being there every day and they want to micromanage every detail and every bit of tile that gets laid and every piece of drywall that goes up and every brushstroke on the wall. Really, you don't need to do that.

Ideally, with my investments, the fewer times I can see them, the better. So if I only need to go to a house four times to get it done, then I'll only go to a house four times in order to get a rehab done. I really don't want to have to spend extra time there.

People don't realize all the different hands that can be involved in this. When you manage a house project for an investor, you take away their having to deal with the tile people, the roofers and the electricians.

If we we're talking about a theoretical average flip job in Houston, how many different trades would the average investor have to manage?

Chris Adkins: On average, there is no simple, run-of-the-mill rental rehab. There can be anywhere from six to eight trades on a given job. And first, it's communicating with them what you want and managing them and their time, and making sure they get the right materials on time and they're focusing on getting the desired outcome.

But more than that, it's about finding quality people that can work labor-wise on the cheaper end of the spectrum, but quality-wise, they're in the middle.

Because there are a lot of guys out there that are really cheap that have very poor quality, and then there are a lot of guys out there that are really expensive that have really great quality that you don't necessarily need.

It's about finding those guys in the middle. And that's where we try to be. –The subcontractors we want are medium-priced and medium-to-high quality.

People don't realize that as a contractor, you don't just understand how to measure how much carpet you need or how many buckets of paint you're going to need.

You actually look at the investor's goal for that property.

Could their remodeling or renovation budget be drastically different if they're flipping a house than if they are going to hold that house long-term as a rental?

Chris Adkins: Yes. Absolutely. That's one of the first things we ask any customer that we're going to work with or bid a job for. We ask them what their intended goal is with this project. Are they looking for a high-end flip or are they looking for it to be a middle-of-the-road rental?

That's definitely going to determine the budget because not only do your labor and your materials costs climb if you get into the higher quality and the higher end houses, but the time it takes to complete that and the scope of work itself can increase.

Sometimes there are sewer lines or roofs that you may not replace if you're going to rent the house because they've got another good four or five years left on them. But if you're going to flip that house, you want to let people know that you have a brand new this or that and not that it's towards the end of its lifetime.

Let's say you have the exact same house in a neighborhood priced at $150,000.

What are the key differences you would see if someone plans on renting that house out or if someone is going to flip that house or turn it for retail?

Chris Adkins: When it comes to renting at that price point, we're looking a lot more for durability. So we might do a different type of flooring. We might do ceramic tile throughout the entire common area of the house and then only do carpet in the bedrooms.

And we're also looking for longevity and durability, even down to the paint. So the type of paint we use would be different. It would be a little bit less expensive.

There are also other things that would be different, such as the tub surround, the actual tubs and shower kits we use, and some of the light fixtures. We use a different line of light fixtures for rentals versus flips.

And some of the hardware like doorknobs, doorstops and plumbing fixtures are less expensive. There are certain things you can get away with in a rental that are less expensive things that still look quite nice, but they're far more durable.

Whereas with a flip, you're really trying to go not so much for longevity, but with perceived value. So you want to use pricier things, such as a little more expensive flooring. We have a laminate product that we use. It's a little bit more expensive than tile, but it looks a lot better in a finished product. We just don't really trust its durability for a rental. So that's something we put in flips that we don't put in rentals.

The same thing applies with the light fixtures and the plumbing fixtures. They're a little bit upgraded and we're not as concerned with durability and longevity. For a rental, we're really concerned about longevity and durability because we don't want to have to replace them every time we do a make ready.

The decisions that an investor makes in a remodel, especially if they're going to hold something as a rental, could have long-lasting consequences on the maintenance and upkeep of that home.

When tenants move out, a lot of investors get some big surprises. The house may not always be left in a condition where it just needs to be swept and rented, right?

Chris Adkins: That's right. You go into a decent rental, if you're cash-flowing $300 a month, that's roughly $3,600 a year, assuming no major incidents or no major repairs need to be done during that time.

So if the average tenant stays for two to three years, you're only averaging $6,000 to $9,000.

Let's say on the high end, you average $10,000 cash flow in that three-year time. If you go in and you have to paint a 1500 square foot house and redo all the flooring, you can cut into that $10,000 profit pretty quickly. It starts eating it up depending on the quality of your tenants and the durability and the longevity of the products you used in the home.

Right. And that's where fear comes in for a lot of investors. Some don't know if they're judging things correctly.

What are some rules of thumb that investors can use when they walk through a house to start tallying up potential costs before they get too committed into a purchase?

Chris Adkins: We have the short, medium and long way of estimating.

The short way is looking at the overall condition of the house. We figure if it's just paint and carpet and a couple of light fixtures here and there, you can get that done for about $9 to $12 a square foot.

If it's paint, carpet, all the light fixtures, some additional flooring and some plumbing fixtures, that's in the $12 to $15 a square foot range.

If you start adding some exterior repairs, significant painting, drywall patching, re-texturing, all the light fixtures, all the flooring, countertops, tub surrounds, you're getting into that $15 to $20 a square foot range.

That doesn't include what we call the Big Four, which are roof, foundation, A/C and concrete.

So if I went into a house and the roof was okay, the foundation was okay, and there is no major concrete that was needed, the A/C is in good condition, and all it needs is a paint job and little flooring, I can estimate that I can get that done for $4 or $5 a square foot, because I'm going to have to do a lot of prepping. If it needed more flooring or some lighting, I'd be in the $8 a square foot range.

Your company is known for how quickly you can do estimates on homes that are pretty accurate.

How many houses have you done over the years to be able to acquire this type of data to allow you to do this?

Chris Adkins: I've been with the company 3½ years. My first year there, I was part of 86 projects. In my second year, we did slightly more. And then we slowed down here a little bit recently. So I've consulted on well over 250 projects.

Our owner and founder, Brant Phillips, has been doing this about seven or eight years. I want to say he averages about 70 to 75 projects a year where he's either doing the projects that he invests in, his rentals and his flips, and also doing customer projects. So he's actually probably closer to 600 or 700 rehab projects that he's been a part of, not including things he's just consulted on.

Based on that volume of data, we have some really good formulas put together where we know if we measure that it's this many inches, it's going to cost us exactly this for this type of material and we can be pretty dead-on accurate.

We say we're usually within about 5 or 6%. So we're usually within our budget by 5% or we may go over about 5%. But we're within 5% accurate.

Those are remarkable numbers.

New investors usually have fears that crop up as they're looking at getting that first property.

What are the most common fears you see where people may move from making logical decisions to emotional or fear-based decisions, when they're getting into a project?

Chris Adkins: It's usually one of two things. Right now, the market is so good that there are a lot of great deals out there and it's really a seller's market. So we're pushing price points everywhere. One of the problems that fosters is that investors fall in love with the house and they want it to be perfect. They want it to have everything.

So a lot of the times, they want to over-rehab it and they want to do too much to it. We have to tell them it's a seller's market. So that means you don't have to necessarily be perfect. No house can possibly have everything. It just can't. It's limited by the laws of physics.

So we see a lot of people fall in love with houses when they have good deals and end up wanting to do too much.

Then we see a lot of people try to cut corners out of fear, when they realize they're into a bad deal. They try to put less money into the house than they really should and it ends up costing them more in the long run. That's a call we probably have at our company once a week to once every other week.

We'll go out and bid on a job and then somebody else will bid against us. They'll end up going with another company because the estimate is $2,000 or $3,000 cheaper. We wish them luck on the project.

Then they'll come back a month or two months later and tell us their contractor is way over budget. Even through they thought the other contractor would be cheaper than us, they've already spent more and he's not finishing the job. Then they need us to come back and fix it.

A lot of times, unfortunately, you can't help those people because they're already way over budget and it's going to cost us more to fix poor workmanship than it would for them to just finish it and take their lumps. We say, "We'll get you on the next one."

You bring up a good point about investors over-remodeling projects.

You make recommendations to your clients that actually cut into your own profits. The great thing about your business model is you are looking for long-term clients because these are investors that will buy house after house.

What's the reaction from investors when you actually suggest doing something that would make you less money in the short-term?

Chris Adkins: A lot of their reaction is they want to do it anyway. But one of the things that I bring up is I can sell you construction. If you just want me to come in and sell you construction, I can build you a house with a waterfall in the living room and golden toilets and all that in the bathroom.

I can sell you the most construction I can possibly sell you on one project and I may make $10,000 to $15,000 on that project. And then you're out of business because you've lost your shirt on that house. Or even if you're not out of business, you never want to work with me again.

Versus I can sell you the amount of construction that you need and make less, but I can do that several times over because you're going to keep being successful on your investment. My goal is to sell you a product that's going to make you money and make a return on your investment. So then you're going to want to come back and work with us again. You know we're trying to do right by you.

A lot of times, I shock people in our meetings. I'm the worst salesman ever because the last thing I want to do is sell construction. I've told several clients, you may not even need us to do this. You may just need a really good cleaning and you can rent this house out.

Well, that really identifies why a lot of smart investors will use Invest Home Pro. They're hiring you because of the result they know they can get by using you because of your reliability and your knowledge about investment.

What is the most common mistake people make in their decisions to overdo a property? What element of a house are you commonly making recommendations that people back off of?

Chris Adkins: Definitely the kitchen and the master bathroom. Those are the two areas of the house that are going to sell the house for you. Nobody walks into a house and says, "I hate the kitchen. I hate the master bathroom. But I really love this front bedroom closet, so I'll take it."

It's usually those two areas that they're going to fall in love with. That's where you see a lot of people overspending.

The other thing is that people don't understand there's a cumulative effect for every decision you make. This project is not just one conglomerate thing. It's a series of several hundred smaller decisions.

You can make those decisions in such a way that instead of going for the highest-priced or the shiniest object on every decision, you can go for the medium price, the medium product on most decisions and pick one or two high-end items. And when they come together, the cumulative effect is that they will have a high-end look.

A lot of people don't understand that cumulative effect and we'll dig into a project with them and they'll want to come in and start changing things in the kitchen and the bathroom.

They just don't realize that every time they make one of those decisions to change something, they're adding $100 here and $100 there, which isn't a big deal. But in the long run, when you make 60, 70, 100 decisions over the course of a project, then that can vastly affect your budget.

A lot of people see the reality shows and they see people somehow manage to work their way out of problems. They think a lot of investing is based on gut or instinct.

When you have access to numbers, would you work based on gut or instinct?

Chris Adkins: No, because data can be your friend. I don't want to get inundated by it, but you need just the right analysis in just the right spots and that will allow you to make the key decisions. Everything isn't really irrelevant, but it doesn't have as large of an effect as you would think.

People have a fear of their inability to find contractors that are trustworthy or are reliable when they decide to run their own projects to save money.

Are there any secrets to finding those contractors and not letting them get ahead of you on payments or time?

Chris Adkins: Yes. And they don't realize that their time may be better spent by raising cheaper money or finding the next deal or doing the next thing in their business.

But as far as subcontractors go, a general rule of thumb that we follow is we don't care how good of a marketer you are or how many reviews you have on Angie's List or whatever. We want a referral-based contractor.

So we ask a lot of our fellow investors, a lot of our friends and a lot of guys that we know that are in the business to refer trades when we need a specific one. A new investor can do that, as well.

If they're a realtor and are familiar with investing, if they have a hard money lender they're familiar with for investing, if they have anybody like a mentor or someone else they know that's an investor, they can always ask them for references.

And that's one of the key things that I want to hear is that another investor has used this subcontractor and had a good experience with them.

And then, yes, you hit the nail on the head, as far as money goes. Even with general contractors, we definitely work on a draw system. You never get paid until a job is done. I realize a lot of people get hesitant to give people a first draw, but that's necessary to get the work done.

Sometimes, unfortunately, people do get burned on that first draw, where they go and they write a check to get the job started and the subcontractor or the general contractor closes up shop and leaves town.

But that's why we take referrals very highly and very seriously, over just who the best guy is that did Google Pay Per Click or Facebook ads.

That's important for people to know that would like to do it themselves. You have several clients that were prior "do it yourselfers," right? They learned very quickly that that's not the way to run a profitable investment.

Chris Adkins: Yes. We've even learned that lesson. We originally started this company because we didn't want to be painting houses on the weekend and trying to lay tile on Friday night.

That's a lesson a lot of newer investors have to learn the hard way. It's like if you have kids. You can tell them a hundred thousand times don't touch the stove because it's hot. But they're not going to listen until they put their hand on the stove and they realize, wow, I don't want to do that again.

So as much as we do with coaching and trying to help new investors, we can tell them you don't want to manage the job yourself. But, eventually, they have to try it and they have to do it on their own and they almost have to have a bad experience. And I'm not saying that they all do have a bad experience, or that I want them to. I'm just saying that's the unfortunate reality of construction.

Once most investors go through that on their first project, they're very eager to work with general contractors.

I lump that together in a call that we get pretty regularly. That's the call we get all the time, where we give a guy a bid and he says, no, it's too expensive. I'll manage it myself and save the extra $4,000 or $5,000 that we're making on that project. And he'll call us three or four weeks later and just say, "Help. I'm in trouble. I'm way over budget and I'm not even half-way done."

Unfortunately, at that point, usually the damage is already done on that project. So we're in there just trying to save the ship.

One of the things that are incredibly valuable and unique are you also have both an educational and a consultative component to what you do.

Some clients may choose to go on their own, but they hire you on a consulting basis up front. Explain the other educational and consultative components that Invest Home Pro has.

Chris Adkins: Teaching people and showing people how to properly run their investments so they can make money is almost more fun for me.

One of the things we do is we consult by the hour. If people have a project that they want an estimate on that's not under contract, or that they're thinking about managing themselves, we can come out and give them a very thorough estimate. So they have a scope of work to guide them along the project.

And then, we can also touch base with them throughout the project, just to make sure they're not running into any snafus and not running into the very common problems that first-time or second-time project managers run into. We lend them our experience, while not necessarily lending them our direct project management skills, our subcontractors, our software and all that.

We can just lend them our experience and let them know, hey, you're doing well on this, but you need to watch out for this. Or see what's happening over here. That's a very easy fix. Or we can do this over here. And just give them a little bit of experience so they can see the road ahead and avoid some of the pitfalls and potholes.

What do you think is the difference in investors who have a scarcity mindset when hiring service providers, versus those who don't?

Chris Adkins: The difference, and you hit the nail on the head, is scarcity. It comes down to there are some investors who, because they choose to manage their own project and they choose to cut corners and try to save a dollar here, they're tripping over the tens of thousands of dollars that can be found in doing more deals, raising better money to make your deals more profitable, and just generally having more free time, pick up a few pennies here and there.

A lot of those investors that want to manage their own projects and want to get deeply involved in how the electrical is going in and how the tiles are getting laid, they miss out. They may save the $2,000 or $3,000 in management fees and miss out on the $20,000 or $30,000 from doing several extra deals a year.

We have a pretty deep client base of investors that use us consistently and repeatedly to the point where it's almost hard for us to accept new customers sometimes.

Those investors understand that by handing over the keys and leaving it to us and coming back to put a sign in the yard, they can maximize their time and be doing several more deals a year and other projects and other things to make money.

Versus trying to save, to be honest, what's a very marginal markup for the most part, on our construction cost.

So it's basically just leveraging our time and our experience to get what they want done anyway.

I would say one of the reasons I work for this company is it was already established when I started getting into the investment world in Houston. And I recognized that it was one of the better companies for construction and education. So that's one of the reasons I work here.

And even if I didn't work here, I would probably still use this company to do my rehabs, even if I had to pay them a couple of extra bucks for management fees. Just because I do know the reputation and I do know the quality of the work they do.

So it's easy for me to say here's an extra couple of thousand dollars for each project to manage it and handle it so that I never have to see it. And I can go focus on doing more deals and doing more projects and having more money to make those more profitable.

How can people find out more about Chris Adkins, Invest Home Pro, and how to get involved?

Chris Adkins: They can visit our website, which is www.InvestHomePro.com. We have an "About" section on the website where you can learn about our company.

But, more importantly, we have the "Bid Request" section, which is on the top right-hand of the page. So if they have a project they have under contract that they want us to go out and give them an estimate on, they can do that.

Or they can submit a house for a consultation. If they don't have it under contract or they just want us onsite as a consultant to help them on the project and suggest designs and features or finishes or all that stuff, we can do that.

About Chris Adkins

Chris works full-time in real estate as an investor and adviser on projects. He has a deep understanding of trends in the many submarkets in and around Houston and specializes in renovation estimating and project analysis. He has learned the 'ins and outs' of construction and how to maximize flip and rental opportunities. He coaching students as well as educating and advocating for the many clients of Invest Home Pro.

Prior to joining the Invest Home Pro team, Chris served honorably in the United States Army for six years and preformed multiple overseas tours. He uses the discipline, leadership, teamwork and critical thinking skills gained during his service to assist the Invest Home Pro team in multiple ways.

Business Name: Invest Home Pro

Website: InvestHomePro.com

Facebook: Facebook.com/Chris.Adkins.1614460

LinkedIn: LinkedIn.com/pub/Chris-Adkins/89/974/a83

INSURANCE AGENT

Sal Ortiz specializes in insurance for real estate investors. Most investors don't realize that many insurance policies will not protect their best interests for the many events that can impact a property.

In this chapter, Sal discusses the many natural and man-made events that can trigger the need for coverage within an insurance policy. He points out the policies that do and do not cover many of these events. Most investors are not aware that the most common occurrence is a water or plumbing leak and many policies do not cover this.

Sal is an expert at helping investors determine the best coverage to meet the many needs they may have with investment properties, whether they're flipping those properties or holding them long-term as rentals.

He discusses some attention-grabbing issues that will have everyone reaching out to read their policies.

Conversation with Sal Ortiz

People that are buying property to hold for rentals are different from people that are buying distressed property that needs rehabbing for flipping and selling retail.

Insurance can be complicated when it comes time to decide what kind of insurance you need based on the strategy that you are using for your investments, is that correct?

Sal Ortiz: That's correct. In Texas, there is no standard policy that you can get. Every company writes their own policy and the Department of Insurance simply approves the policy for that particular carrier.

So just because one carrier may offer a policy for vacant houses doesn't mean that everybody is going to offer that. Also, if they're with different carriers, the policy that you or your neighbor has may be completely different.

Since property policies in Texas are now individually written by the carriers, you have to be careful and make sure you understand your policy. You need to ask questions to ensure that whatever is important for you is, in fact, covered by that policy and provided by that carrier.

That's an important point. Many times, people make the mistake of asking blanket questions when they're looking at service providers. You've probably been asked if you carry policies for real estate investors.

Sal Ortiz: Yes. Investors need to ask more specific questions.

For instance, you could have a policy which many carriers offer called a Texas Dwelling Policy - Form 3, TDP-3 and it's going to be a very comprehensive type policy.

But different carriers offer different versions of that TDP-3, which in Texas is probably one of the most comprehensive policies for investors and for landlords. You'll have some TDP-3's that do include water damage in case there's a plumbing leak. But you'll also have other TDP-3's that do not include that important coverage.

And that can be a big surprise for people, right?

Sal Ortiz: Yes, it really can. So there are a lot of nuances in each particular policy. Just because you have a TDP-3 and your neighbor has a TDP-3, if they're with different carriers, they will probably have different coverages and different endorsements that are attached to it.

So it's important to make sure that you ask a lot of questions and that you have a very good relationship with your agent so that you can ask questions of as they come up.

At the same time, whenever you're establishing that relationship, find out what's important to you. If price is the main motivator, which it is to a lot of investors, and you just want to be covered for the major perils, then you'll be able to be afforded coverage with just about anybody.

On the other hand, you want something a little bit more comprehensive and you might want to make sure that in case something happens you don't have any issues as far as coverage is concerned. In that case, it's important that you make the time and sit down with your agent and review those coverages, the details, and ask as many questions as possible.

There's a saying that is especially true when it comes to real estate investing. "The people that don't need more comprehensive coverage are the people that nothing's happened to yet."

Sal Ortiz: Yes, that's probably true. I like that.

Let's talk about the types of coverage that are available. Vacant property insurance is very important to investors, so let's start there.

What types of insurance options do they need to consider having for that time that their property is vacant?

Sal Ortiz: That's a very important question because vacancy is defined differently by different carriers.

Most carriers will define vacancy as when at least 50% of its livable contents have been removed from the house or the property. And they will have different dates. So some of them will say 50% of the livable contents have been removed from the property and the property is now vacant for over 30 days, 60 days, or a maximum of 90 days. Then the house is considered vacant.

Once it's vacant, there is little to no coverage afforded to the property. You're paying the monthly premiums or you've paid for the year. But there may be no coverage for vandalism, fire, liability, etc., if the property is, in fact, vacant.

So it's important to find out what the vacancy clause states as far as number of days. How long can the house be with the contents removed without it being vacant? Is it 30, 60 or 90 days?

And how strict is their definition of vacancy? Because if a home does become vacant, then you need to make sure that they add a vacancy clause endorsement to the policy, which may extend coverages like liability, fire and vandalism.

Most people may not be aware that if their rental is vacant for an extended period of time, there could actually be a window of time when they're not covered.

What are some of the problems that could happen during that timeframe?

Sal Ortiz: That is a huge issue and it's a huge issue for agents, as well, because this is probably one of the main reasons that agents are sued for what's termed Errors and Omissions. An E&O may be brought against an agent when the client comes back and says no one ever told me. Or the agent knew or the staff knew that I was going to be renovating the house. So it's a big issue all the way around and you don't want to get involved with that.

The best thing to do is ask questions. Know exactly what your policy is affording as far as vacancy is concerned. It's one of the primary questions you should ask whenever you're buying a policy. As an investor, you may have a time frame in mind to either turn this around in less than a month or in less than two months. How much time do you have before that property becomes vacant?

To add a vacancy endorsement on any policy is an expensive proposition. It normally doubles and sometimes triples the price of the policy because of the risk.

Everybody knows a vacant home is much more susceptible to vandalism. If there's a small fire in a vacant home, it can become a larger fire. An insurance company knows the inherent risk in vacant property, and they're going to price for it.

Even when someone has vacancy insurance, there are still different variables to consider, such as the distinction between theft and vandalism.

What are some of those nuances in coverages?

Sal Ortiz: For example, if someone steals the outside unit of the A/C or they take the copper wiring from the outside unit.

Most would consider someone stealing the A/C unit as theft. However, most insurance companies consider stealing the outside unit as vandalism. If they damage or remove the copper, that is still considered by most companies as a vandalism.

As opposed to when someone went inside the house and stole the refrigerator or washer and dryer. Then that is considered theft and most of the investor type policies will not cover that.

So there is a fine line as to what insurance companies determine to be theft versus what they would determine to be vandalism.

Any type of personal property would most likely not be covered because most of your investor type policies, most of your landlord policies, and most of your Texas Dwelling Policies, Form 1, Form 2 and Form 3 in Texas do not afford Theft.

They will afford vandalism if you add it by endorsement. But they will not afford theft. If someone steals a refrigerator, or a TV, more than likely coverage will not be applicable.

But if they vandalize, if they break the door, break the glass, or actually steal something that's permanently attached, a lot of times they will afford coverage for that. A few carriers in the marketplace now offer a "Burglary" endorsement. This endorsement will afford theft of personal property when forced entry is present.

Talk about natural perils because we certainly have some of those in the Houston area that people need to be aware of. One of the big ones that people overlook is flood insurance.

Talk about the risk and benefits of considering flood insurance, particularly on rental homes over the long term. Sometimes people make that decision based on whether the property is in the flood plain or not.

Sal Ortiz: Exactly. The number one concern for most investors is if the property is in a flood zone and that's very easy to find out. An agent should be able to figure that out quickly with no cost incurred to the investor.

It's either inside or outside the flood zone. If it's outside the flood zone, then most investors will decide not to buy flood insurance.

However, I'll give you an example. When Tropical Storm Allison hit Houston in June of 2001, 40% of the homes that were flooded by Allison in the Houston area were outside the flood zone.

So there are still properties that are damaged to a great extent by flood, even if they're outside the flood zone. Being outside the flood zone does not automatically mean that you will not be flooded.

Even though there have been improvements to bayous after Allison in the Houston area, the fact is there are still large portions of Houston that are susceptible to flooding, both inside and outside the flood area.

Preferred flood policies for properties that are outside the flood zone are quite inexpensive and provide peace of mind for flooding. You might pay $430 a year for a $250,000 policy for property outside the flood zone.

One question that a lot of folks ask is the definition of flooding. If a pipe breaks and it floods the inside of a house, is that flooding? That will not meet the definition of flooding. Flooding is defined as rising water that comes from the street and into your home.

This is as opposed to a plumbing leak that damages and floods the house. That would be covered by your hazard policy and by your landlord policy, if the water endorsement was added.

Peace of mind is one of the best investments a lot of investors make. They buy flood insurance, even though they're outside the flood zone for their peace of mind.

Sal Ortiz: They expanded and improved a lot of the bayous and they put hundreds of millions of dollars into that project here in Harris County. However, as a result of that project, some folks that were not in the flood zone are now in flood zones.

So it's always important to ask if you're in a flood zone and once you find out, figure out what the price is and hopefully it's still within your budget to buy that peace of mind.

I think having flood insurance is definitely important. Even though you may think you're well protected, there will be another Tropical Storm Allison that sits over Harris County for five to six days. Who knows what will happen?

Well, if it does happen to you, you'll find that that's the best $25-30 a month you spent on that house.

Pipes bursting are another one of those things that may or may not be covered.

Sal Ortiz: That's correct. There are various types of policies here in Texas that afford water coverage to rental dwellings or investment type properties.

The most standard policies which are offered by most carriers are what are called the Texas Dwelling Form. A Texas Dwelling Policy - Form 1, Form 2 and Form 3.

The Form 3 is going to be the only one that's going to afford water coverage. But even some Form 3 policies exclude water. So if you're interested in securing a comprehensive policy, ask for the Texas Dwelling Form 3, and ensure that plumbing leaks and water are, in fact, covered.

Another insurance company may call the Texas Dwelling - Form 3 policy a Landlord Package Policy (LPP). Ask your agent if they carry that. And then simply ask, "Is this the policy that's going to afford plumbing leak coverage?" Because that's the number one peril. It's not hurricanes. It's not hail. It's not even theft. The number one peril for most property losses is plumbing leaks.

Talk about liability because liability is outside of vandalism, theft or other perils. There is a lot of latitude as to what can happen with liability.

What are some liability examples that landlords or people that are in the renovation process face and what are some protections they can take?

Sal Ortiz: If you're looking to afford a comprehensive plan, you definitely have to include Liability. Even if you don't really care for the coverage for water and you don't want to pay for that risk, you should definitely consider purchasing a Liability endorsement.

There are only a few policies that afford a Liability endorsement in Texas. The Texas Dwelling - Form 1 policy does not afford Liability. The Texas Dwelling - Form 2 policy does not afford Liability. The TDP-3, the Texas Dwelling - Form 3 policy does afford Liability. So you want to make sure you have that.

The other form, otherwise known as the Landlord Package Policy, will also afford Liability.

Liability can be as simple as the tenant has a dog and the tenant's dog bit the neighbor. So you figure why am I responsible? As the investor and the owner of the property, it's not my dog.

But then all of a sudden, the neighbor gets an attorney and the attorney feels that there was a rotted piece of wood on the fence that should have been fixed, and that's the liability of the owner. So they'll cast a wide net and they'll see what they can get.

Liability is definitely an important coverage that an investor should consider, either with the Texas Dwelling - Form 3 or a Landlord Package Policy.

Or, if your agent doesn't offer Liability in any type of tenant policy, then you could go to another plan that's called a Comprehensive Personal Liability Policy. It's a standalone Liability policy, otherwise known as a CPL. A Comprehensive Personal Liability Policy will allow you to put two, three or four properties under one policy.

That policy only covers one thing and one thing only, which is Liability to your properties as an investor. So if you have one, two, three or four properties, you can put them all on one policy under a CPL and that's a very important thing to do and to consider.

Is an umbrella policy something that would be considered, or is that something different?

Sal Ortiz: That's something different because the umbrella is a secondary policy. Meaning that an umbrella policy will generally not be primary.

I gave the example where the tenant's dog bit the neighbor and then brought a cause against you as the owner because of the fact that there was a rotted board or a hole in the fence that wasn't fixed and you should have known about it. If you have Liability on your primary policy, which is the Landlord Package Policy, or your TDP-3, that policy will afford the liability towards that claim.

However, if that claim is a serious claim, now instead of it being a $100,000, $200,000 or $300,000 loss and you're sued and it's a half a million or a million dollar loss, then the Umbrella picks up everything above the first $300,000.

Generally, Umbrella policies are not very expensive. They're priced low because they're not the primary policy in case of loss. They're the secondary policy in case of loss. They only pay once the primary limits have been exhausted.

A CPL is a primary policy. And the reason the CPL is generally priced low is because they only cover one thing – Liability. They won't afford any coverage for theft or vandalism. So if the policy you bought does not come with Liability, go out and seek a CPL.

You may want to get extra protection for major losses. Someone may be severely hurt and they blame you for not having proper lighting. Or they blame you for not fixing the stairs outside or the railing outside and someone has tripped. If you want to have that extra protection, then on top of the CPL and on top of the Liability that you have on your primary policy, you should ask your agent for an Umbrella policy.

One thing people need to understand is that smart investors who use the services of a team don't consider it an expense. They consider it something that is protecting a very important piece of their lives – their investments and their future financial well-being.

Can you give an example to illustrate the importance of being properly insured?

Sal Ortiz: I gave you the example of the dog bite because that's a case that happened to one of our clients. Our investor had a property on which the tenant's dog bit a young lady, the daughter of the neighbor. And the case was brought against our insured, our client. We were able to defend it because he did have a policy with Liability.

We were able to win the case because there was no negligence proven against our client. When you have Liability as part of your coverage, it will likely afford defense at dollar one. The insurance company will actually hire the attorney for you and defend you, where you don't have to come up with that risk, regardless of if you were negligent or not negligent. The fact is you have someone to defend you.

So it's important to ask questions. Even if you've established a great relationship with your agent, ask questions. Take the time and find out. It's the wrong time to find out at the time of loss. No one at the time of loss likes surprises. You want to know that what you're paying for is exactly what you thought you were getting.

What is the most common and general protection for a landlord that's buying multiple properties and they're building up a portfolio? And are there cost benefits when you insure multiple properties?

Sal Ortiz: There are. A lot of insurers will give you discounts for the number of properties that you add. The other thing that we haven't talked about is how these properties are styled. Are they all under an individual name? Are they under an LLC?

If there's an LLC involved and you're buying the properties under an LLC or S corporation or C corporation, then the corporation is actually the owner of the properties. You're leaving the personal line side of the business and you're going to a commercial exposure that just simply adds another layer of insurance and matters that need to be addressed.

A lot of personal line carriers will generally not insure an investor property that's styled as an LLC. They'll insure it as a commercial property. You leave the personal lines market and go into something completely different.

How it's styled, is it one property or is it two – all these things are important. Do you want to have the most comprehensive coverage? Do you want the exposure for water covered? Do you want the exposure for Liability covered?

There's another issue that we haven't talked about. A lot of these policies that are sold in Texas for investors only cover actual cash value. They do not afford replacement cost.

So, if there is a storm that damages the roof and the roof needs to be repaired because of the hail damage, will they pay replacement cost value and not depreciate the value of this old roof?

Or will they actually take depreciation and only pay the depreciated value of the roof? You need to find that out.

That's a very important point. If someone has a 20-year-old roof and the life of a roof is 30 years, when Tropical Storm Leopold comes through, a lot of people think they'll get a new roof. Is that the case?

Sal Ortiz: You have to be careful because most investors want the lowest priced policy they can get away with.

And those policies do not afford replacement cost. When you get those policies, any damage that's done to that house is going to be paid at actual cash value, whether it's vandalism or a natural occurrence.

So if you have a 30-year roof on that house and it is 20 years old, 2/3 of the roof has been aged and is already gone. If it costs $10,000 to replace that roof, they're going to pay you 33% of that cost. 67% of the replacement cost is deducted.

You'll get a check for $3,300 minus your deductible. If you have $1,000 or $2,000 deductible then you're getting very little for that $10,000 roof.

So you need to determine whether your policy affords replacement cost or actual cash value. And if it affords replacement cost, is it replacement for just natural occurrences? Or is it replacement cost for things like water leaks or vandalism?

Every policy is different. Just because one company offers a Landlord Package Policy doesn't mean that another company that offers the same thing covers the same thing. It's completely different and that's why it's important to ask questions.

People have to really think about that because, as with the roof example, they might feel they have insurance but what your insurance covers can be quite variable.

Sal Ortiz: By the time they depreciate it and take out the deductible, you're left with a small stipend compared to the price of putting the roof back. Obviously, no one's going to put that roof back with 20 year old shingles. They're going to put it back with a brand new shingle at a higher cost.

So it's critical to determine if the policy affords replacement cost or if it pays actual cash value. Does the policy afford water leaks, plumbing leaks? Does the policy afford Liability? And what is the definition for vacancy?

These are questions that need to be asked on every policy.

The Texas Dwelling Policy - Form 1, which is extremely common, does not afford replacement cost. It's a strict actual cash value policy. No coverage for Liability. No replacement cost and no water.

The Texas Dwelling - Form 2 policy will be exactly the same as the Texas Dwelling Form 1, but the one thing that's different is going to be replacement cost. On the Texas Dwelling - Form 2, you can add replacement cost. It still may not come with Liability and will likely not come with water coverage for plumbing leaks.

Then you could step up to the Form 3, which will give you the most comprehensive coverage. It will give you water, replacement cost and Liability. Obviously, it's more expensive, but you get what you pay for.

And even on the Form 3, you still have to ask questions because there are some Form 3 policies in Texas that just will not afford water (plumbing leaks).

How many landlords out there do you think know off the top of their heads what type of insurance they have?

Sal Ortiz: Probably less than 10% know what the answer to that question is.

How many people, landlords and investors, are walking around right now with a Level 1 policy and would be absolutely shocked and probably in some very serious financial peril if something happened and they thought they were covered?

Sal Ortiz: I would imagine the vast majority of them would be. What I find a lot is that people will say, "I just want to be covered for the major perils. Give me coverage for wind. Give me coverage for natural occurrences. Give me coverage for fire.

And let's buy a CPL policy on the side to cover three or four of my properties. Because the Comprehensive Personal Liability policy is pretty inexpensive because they only cover Liability."

So a lot of them will do that. They'll get a combination. They'll get the Form 1 plus the CPL and they understand there's no replacement cost or water coverage. They're willing to take that risk.

There is no coverage for plumbing leaks, which is, again, the number one peril. But that's a small thing. It's just sheetrock and new carpeting. I'm okay with that. But cover me for the hurricane. Cover me for the fire. Cover me for the stolen A/C. But don't cover me for the small stuff.

Everybody's budget is different. The way I approach it is it's my job to explain the options. It's your job to decide what you want. But at least what we do is we give you options. And the more questions you ask, the more knowledgeable you'll be, no matter who you're dealing with.

It's important for folks that are reading this book to understand that they need to make sure that they take the time to ask their agent questions to ensure that they're getting exactly what they want, because there is something out there for everybody.

If someone's thinking about purchasing property and getting into buying rental properties or they have properties right now and they're thinking they don't know what kind of insurance they have, what's the first thing they should do? Call their agent or get out the paperwork and figure out what it is they have?

Sal Ortiz: They should take the time to read their policy because today's policies are supposed to be in an easy, readable form. So they're not as complicated as they used to be ten or fifteen years ago to read and understand. And even though some parts are still complicated, they'll take coverage away and then they'll give it back with another clause and endorsement.

You can also call your agent. Sit down with your agent and make the time to review what you have. You've invested a lot of money in this property. You've invested a lot of time and effort into doing what you do as far as your investments. You want to make sure you're protected.

How can people get in touch with you and find out more about you to take advantage of the knowledge and the expertise you have about insurance?

Sal Ortiz: We welcome a lot of investors. We have very different types of policies that we offer and something for just about everybody.

They can get in touch with me by phone at 281-587-0000. Or they can reach me by email at SalOrtiz@allstate.com.

About Sal Ortiz

As a Personal Financial Representative in Houston, I know many local families. My knowledge and understanding of the people in this community help me provide customers with an outstanding level of service. I look forward to helping families like yours protect the things that are important – your family, home, car and more. I can also help you prepare a strategy to achieve your financial goals.

Business Name: Sal Ortiz – Allstate Insurance

Website: Allstate.com/SalOrtiz

Facebook: Facebook.com/OrtizInsurance.Allstate

LinkedIn: LinkedIn.com/in/OrtizSal

Twitter: @Ortiz_Insurance

HOME STAGING

Rhonda Conchola creates magic within the real estate industry. As a home stager, when she puts her artistic skills to work, her design concepts bring a house together in a way that tugs at the heart strings of potential buyers.

She helps Houston real estate investors add value to their properties without changing the structure of the homes. Rhonda creates a beautiful design concept using an inventory of home furnishings, accessories, wall art, silk plants, trees, and bedding. She has a dream warehouse full of great items. In addition to working with investors, she also helps builders, realtors, contractors and homeowners.

Investors realize many benefits when they use the expertise and knowledge of a home stager. While fewer days on the market and a higher selling price may be common knowledge, some other benefits of staging will surprise you.

Rhonda shares some very practical information that will benefit both seasoned and new practitioners in the real estate investment industry, improving your return on investment.

Conversation with Rhonda Conchola

As a home stager, you take something that is ordinary and turn it into something extraordinary using your vision of how a home should be staged. You can transform a house from "This isn't bad" to "Wow, this is it! This is the place!"

Please explain exactly what home staging is.

Rhonda Conchola: Home Staging is marketing the home through interior decorating. Most stagers don't put as much focus on interior design as much as they will on who your most likely buyer is and the home's greatest functionality.

It defines the space for potential buyers. It paints a beautiful picture and allows them to come into the home and see something that presents a lifestyle image they can relate to and immediately fall in love with it. It often generates an emotional buying response.

You see a lot of that on the home flipping shows where people know instantly that they want a house. It's almost like you have the ability to hit that dopamine button in people's heads because it really is about coming in and having them fall in love.

Rhonda Conchola: Exactly, and the reason why is because you've already done your homework as a stager before coming into the home. You've analyzed the neighborhood, the area, the size of the home, and the style of the home. You have an idea of who your buyer is and you stage the home by relating to that buyer.

Sometimes we create little vignettes throughout the home that just grab the buyer's attention and that they can relate to. There are little emotional elements throughout the home and you lay it all out there. You draw a picture for them where they can envision exactly how well they're going to "fit" into the home and they just fall in love with it.

Homebuilders and custom homebuilders have been using the concept of home staging for years. Staging allows individual people who are selling homes to level the playing field and use the same persuasion tactics that homebuilders have used for years.

Stagers are very purposeful in how they select and layout the items that they put into there, correct?

Rhonda Conchola: Absolutely. That's something that's been used for some time. In fact, homebuilders are actually moving towards using home stagers quite a bit more now because they see how effective it is. And, in fact, I have several that I've spoken with, and even worked with, that are very interested in staging because it's more cost effective than traditional model home design. They're also able to move their inventory a lot quicker. It's mostly the same concept but a more cost effective value since they are not having to invest several thousands of dollars buying home furnishings and accessories. They now have the option of renting the home stager's items.

Many investors get creative when remodeling a home and start taking walls down or putting them up or making other changes.

You come in after they're done and you make the most of that final product. Sometimes it has a more dramatic effect than some of the things the investors spend a lot of money on.

Talk about how you paint a picture for buyers and show them the potential a house could have.

Rhonda Conchola: Yes sure. I can't tell you how many times I've gone into homes for staging and they've torn down walls and have created this very large and sometimes awkward space. It's great because people love large open spaces and they really want that, however, they often don't really know what to do with it.

They're almost intimidated by this huge open space. It's all open-concept. It's got the kitchen, the dining room, the living room all together, but they're not really sure how to break it down.

So that's what we come in and do. We show them how you can arrange your home office space here and it works great and it's functional. You can do your dining room here and that's awesome. Then, you have this big large living space.

It's all broken down for them and it draws a picture and takes out all the guesswork.

You show people exactly how this home can be used for their purposes. It can be the tipping point that creates a bidding war on a home.

Talk about the outcome that presents when someone does stage a home and the dramatic differences you see in the selling price, the days on the market and the excitement around that home.

Rhonda Conchola: Well, first of all, it's very important to note that the home should be marketed by a great realtor with beautiful online pictures. When the realtor lists the home, it's listed and marketed as a staged home, if it's done properly.

So that creates and generates quite a bit more traffic because realtors want to show a staged home. They don't want to show a home where they have to go in and do all the explaining of how each space works. A staged home does all of that for them.

I think that when people come in and they see that the home's already beautifully decorated with everything very well defined for them, with color and a lifestyle image, there's a quicker buying response. Then your days on market are much less. The excitement or the preliminary marketing before the home actually goes on the market has been done. Finally, the home should be very strategically priced.

And that's the reason that a lot of investors are very successful because all that has all been done. They've pre-marketed the home. They've built that intensity before it even hits the market. They've staged it and they've priced it competitively.

They work with a great realtor and a great marketing team that's done all that for them. That's very important when your goal is to sell it in the least amount of days on the market and for the most amount of money and you want to create bidding wars. That's how I believe you do that.

That definitely explains the value of home staging. Still, many individuals and even investors wonder if it is worth the cost. Smart investors are the ones that are doing this, so the return on the investment of home staging must be dramatic, right?

Rhonda Conchola: Sure, of course! Many people will ask "How much does it cost to do home staging?" I always like to say "Staging is not so much a cost as it is an investment and it should be an unquestionable investment. It should be an integral part of your total renovation plan because there's such a return on it."

The cost is much less than your first price decrease when a house isn't selling. The cost is much less than the five or six months of carrying costs when the house sits on the market for so long because it's not staged or not marketed well. There are statistics everywhere, particularly on www.realtor.org, and www.stagedhomes.com and RESA, the Real Estate Staging Association about the return when you stage a home. They have statistics where they've done studies on it.

The days on market are always less in a staged home than it is on that same home had it not been staged. So, yes, there is an investment but the return is for sure.

The costs of home staging are dwarfed by what it makes for you. I also think about some of the other advantages you mentioned, such as fewer days on market.

Also, if a house doesn't sell right away, some sellers panic and start lowering the price. The seller, however, still has to pay the carrying costs at the same time, don't they?

Rhonda Conchola: That's so true. I've worked with many investors personally that have gone both ways. They started out just listing the home without investing in staging. Then the next time they list, they have talked to other investors who had success with staging and then decide to stage their listing the second time around and have great success with it.

Once they have experienced the difference, they have come to me and said, "Wow. I will never list another home again without immediately staging it first. It's just an amazing difference. It's so integral to the selling process."

At what point in the process should an investor begin considering staging?

Rhonda Conchola: Well, I always recommend doing what I call a pre-flip consultation with a stager. It's very simple. It's basically just walking and talking and going through the home, ideally even before they start the renovation. Going over things with them like what we talked about before, such as where your money would be best invested in doing the updates and what's most important.

Also, at that time, they can plan for what it's going to cost to stage home. If they already know the cost going into the flip then they can plan and set aside that staging budget and have it available and ready when they are done with their renovation.

I think it's a great idea to meet with a stager and walk through the home with the stager before you even get started. A stager can give invaluable information for paint and product selections and other recommendations during the consultation. They can suggest wonderful, easy and practical design conception ideas on how they can best restore the project and be consistent with the design flow, as far as aesthetically.

Right. And I'm aware that stagers can often save a remodeler significant money if they're consulted with ahead of time.

Have you ever had that happen where you've evaluated what an investor wanted to do and pointed out how he could save money by doing something differently and still provide value?

Rhonda Conchola: Absolutely. I've definitely gone through with a few investors and have done that pre-flip consultation with them. Many of them have not quite grasped that concept yet. But it can be so beneficial. And I can tell you the reason why. It's because I've gone into so many homes and they've combined design styles. They don't realize they're doing that because of design inexperience.

The paint colors don't flow. It doesn't go with the flooring they choose or they mix traditional design with contemporary design. There is one color in one room and then another color in a different room. I would have just told them to stick to one color theme and one design style and use it throughout the home. It works great. It gives potential buyers a blank palette. And people love that and it's going to sell quicker than if you were to choose different colors or mixed design styles.

Selling to prospective buyers is completely different than selling to a homeowner. Homeowners will decorate to their own tastes and what they feel defines who they are. This is completely different from staging design for prospective buyers.

Prospective buyers need a blank palette to put their own signature stamp on. It's basically interior design vs. home staging. There's a big difference.

That's part of the psychology of this. You want something that allows all people to fill in the blanks and paint their own picture of what their ultimate home would be, right?

Rhonda Conchola: Yes absolutely. And not to get emotionally tied to what they're doing. Investors will often want to put their signature stamp on the house because they are the ones that purchased and renovated the home. So it's an emotional thing that's very common that investors do.

But at the end of the day, do you really need to invest that much money into extra paint colors? No, not really, because people are going to come in and put whatever colors they want in the house.

It's the same thing even with plumbing fixtures and lighting fixtures. They should have consistent finishes throughout the home because it looks very nice and clean. A lot of times, investors (or worse, the contractor, if they leave the choosing to them) will choose one type of fixture in a space and a different type of fixture in another space and they're completely different from the rest of the fixtures throughout the home.

So it really helps to just talk to a stager. Of course, I think investors really want to own their renovation project and that's great. But it does help to get advice going into the project before you even get started and talk with a stager especially new investors who have never experienced flipping homes before. Allow the stager to present you with very practical design concepts when you're doing your flip and take that knowledge with you to the next flip. You never know what you may learn. The whole idea of going into the flipping business, I believe, is learning to choose your own product selections effectively and this should never be left in the hands of your contractor.

It seems individual homeowners would be more critical than an investor when having a house staged. They may think that a room needs to be configured or decorated a certain way because it's always been that way.

Has a homeowner ever considered not selling, or decided not to sell, after you staged a home for them?

Rhonda Conchola: Yes, and some have told me when they sell this house, I have to come decorate their new home for them.

Actually, I did have one homeowner recently who after I staged their home, fell in love with it all over again and they moved back in. It happens very often to many stagers.

That's remarkable that it can make such a big difference, even for someone who has lived in the home and thinks they know the only ways the furniture can fit in this room.

Sometimes it takes a fresh set of eyes to notice subtle flaws in a house. Even in freshly remodeled homes, there is always a flaw, and it could be a design flaw. A lot of investors get homes with a weird little room in the back or a weird nook – something that's just odd about the home. There are also structural flaws that they just don't have money in their budget to fix.

How can staging accentuate the great things that an investor has done to remodel a home, but also distract from, or lessen, the impact of some of the flaws that a home may have?

Rhonda Conchola: Well, as an example, one investor I recently worked with invested several thousands of dollars in repairing the foundation. It was all done properly and correctly. However, when you walked into the home, you could still feel a little bit of a slant when walking through the living room. So we staged it and brought items in the home where this slant was much less noticeable and it wasn't a problem. The home sold without any foundation issues ever brought up.

That's just one of the many things staging can address. There may be a room that is just really weird and they don't know how to define it. Or this tiny little breakfast area has been brought out now because the walls have been moved and they wonder what they can do with that space that's just so tiny now.

Well, we bring in the perfect sized piece of furniture that's going to define that area. They think it's just so awesome and realize that's what they can use that space for.

So it really defines odd spaces when they're questionable when they don't have anything in them.

Often, people walk into an empty house and think a room seems bigger or smaller when it's empty. It's almost impossible to gauge what it's going to be like with the furniture in there.

What room in a house do you see buyers struggle envisioning how to configure their furniture to fit in that room?

Rhonda Conchola: I think one of the key areas where this is a concern for the homebuyer is the master bedroom. They want to know if their bedroom furniture is going to fit. Well, a lot of times, they won't even know that until they actually get something in there.

And that's what staging does. It brings in the bedroom furniture that shows them they can fit their stuff in there perfectly because they see what's already in there. There is a bed, nightstands, and a really nice little sitting area. It all fits perfect. It'll work for their items. They can see all the extra space left over beyond the queen size bed is going to fit their king size bed and so on.

So that's a big key reason for staging a master bedroom and why we always do that. It is also the same concept in the living and dining areas as well.

Is that just a natural thing with our brains and our concept of space? Is it common for people to think that an empty room seems like it may hold less?

Rhonda Conchola: Absolutely. Even a stager has to come in and measure the space and determine how they're going to lay the space out. It may not look like it's going to fit this or that.

So we have to actually bring the furniture in and place it. Sometimes we will play with it a bit before we actually get it just right. Because when you're dealing with the older homes and the odd layouts, sometimes they're really long and narrow and people don't know where the TV is going to go. How are they going to make this space work as a TV viewing area?

So, we bring in furniture and accessories and even faux TV's to show that this is how you're going to lay out the living area to be perfectly functional and it leaves no room for doubt because it's right there in front of them.

I cannot tell you the number of times I've heard the investors comment "I would have never have thought to set up the room this way, but it looks great!" This is something potential buyers may never have thought of either had the room been left vacant.

A seasoned investor that uses home staging understands the value and will never sell a home without staging. A new investor that's now considering staging their home might see and understand the value, but still can't make the commitment.

What do you see as some of the biggest obstacles that new investors have when they're considering staging?

Rhonda Conchola: Most of the time they think they can't afford it. Or, they didn't really consider it in the beginning, and now towards the end, they're thinking they want to stage but they don't know what it costs or how it works so they never pursue it.

Again, pre-planning is so key. And just really knowing what needs to be done and where they're marketing money needs to go because you have to market your home in order to get it sold quickly. You can't just list it and expect to always have this great outcome.

So staging should always be considered as part of the process and a lot of seasoned investors do that. They don't even think twice about it. It's automatic.

They want to build a portfolio that's impressive. They want to have something, as far as photos, to move forward with when they're going to new banks and lenders with new projects, and even as part of the appraisal process. When staging is there, it also helps to have a more positive outcome with the appraisal process.

This is especially important if you're in an area where it's a very busy investor market. There are certain areas of Houston where we always get staging because it's a very busy investor market and very active.

There are other investors in those areas that are going to be staging and that's your competition. You have to remember that you're competing with other staged houses in today's real estate market because people no longer look at staging as a luxury. It's a necessity.

When you're putting your home on the market without staging, keep in mind you're competing against other staged homes.

As far as choosing a stager, anyone can become a stager, there is no governing agency that licenses stagers. So be sure to check references, get referrals from investors who have used stagers and be sure to view photos of their past staging projects. This will help to determine the experienced stagers and one that will be a great fit for your project.

These days there are some strict guidelines on appraisals. In order to get the profit that they want out of a house, some investors count on that home hitting the top end of the appraisal in that area.

How can staging positively affect an appraisal?

Rhonda Conchola: Well, I'm not real familiar with the appraisal process, but I do know that there are investors that I work with on a regular basis and they insist on staging and leaving that stage in there through the appraisal process because, for whatever reason, it helps. It proves to be helpful for getting that appraisal price that they needed in order to sell the home.

Especially when your goal is to raise the comps and a lot of them do that. Many aggressive investors set goals to raise the comps in a certain area. They want to say that they were able to do that. Having that appraisal come through the way they need it to is key and they insist on having the staging in there.

I believe the reason staging helps is because it adds value to the home. If you bring in several thousand dollars' worth of furniture and accessories and a beautiful design concept, won't the appraiser be impressed with that, as well as the potential homebuyer? Sure! It's made the home more valuable.

Appraisals work by selecting handful of homes in the area and comparing the selling prices. From these, a low-end price and a high-end price, and probably a middle price, can be determined.

An investor wants it to be as easy as possible for the appraiser to match their home up to the high-end comp for that area. When the house stands out to the appraiser, it can help increase the appraised value.

Not all investors consult a home stager before remodeling, or even before listing a home. They think they did everything right. They got their realtor. They took their pictures. They put the sign out and boom, the house is now on the market. Then nothing happens and then they wonder, "Why isn't the house selling?" Then they finally come to you and ask if there is anything that can be done because they have no idea why this house isn't selling.

Have you ever had a situation where you came in at the very end and worked with what has already been done to help sell a house quickly?

Rhonda Conchola: Absolutely. Again, we have to bring in the correct accessorizing that coordinates with what they have done. You go in and you paint a story in each room you stage and you bring the whole house together.

For example, I went into a home recently that I staged that had several different finishes and several different wall colors. It was an investor flipped home.

In my mind as a stager, I'm thinking wow I need to make this house come together because it literally looked like there were so many different finishes and colors throughout the home and it didn't all belong together. That's how it felt. Even my movers noticed the inconsistencies.

When we went in and brought staging into the home, it really just helped tie all the colors together through accessorizing. It had a beautiful design conception and flow, and it sold in a few days after staging. I believe it was because they were noticing the décor and not really focusing any of the inconsistencies.

Anyone who has bought or sold a home understands there is value in your peace of mind when a house sells quickly. If a home doesn't sell quickly, people begin to make decisions based on emotion and fear, rather than based on logic.

Staging alone will not sell a house though. What other factors can affect the time it takes to sell a house?

Rhonda Conchola: I think, because I'm a stager, it's very important to make investors aware of this. It's not always just about the staging. You cannot just stage your home and put it on the market and expect it to sell quickly. It's so important to have all three legs of the chair, so to speak.

You have to have it staged, number one. You have to have it competitively-priced, number two. And number three, you have to have it well-marketed by your realtor. Be sure to ask your realtor what they're doing to market your home. All three of these must work together to get that quick two-day bidding war. Always ask your realtor what his or her marking plan for selling the home? If all they can tell you is that they will get nice pictures and put it up on MLS, you should tell them thank you very much and move along to the next one. Nowadays, there are realtors who have a very creative marketing strategies and a list of things they will do to market the home. Those types always recommend staging because they know the value in it. That's your guy right there! That's the realtor you want.

It's almost like a recipe – if you are missing one of those pieces it can come out very differently.

The return is obvious at this point for someone to work with you, and especially so for those dealing in houses that are $200,000 or above.

If a seller has gone over budget, or is selling a lower-priced home, what would you suggest they do first to get some of the benefits of staging if they have to go in and try it on their own?

Rhonda Conchola: I'm glad you asked because this is very important. You need to paint the home first and foremost. Fresh paint is a must. Make sure it's a neutral paint and you don't have to use more than one color. You don't have to do accent walls. Just go with neutral paints. Neutral paint will take you to the bank. That's what we always tell our clients and it's so very true.

Curb appeal. You can't even get them through the door if they don't like what they see on the exterior of the home. Get your hands dirty. Get out there and manicure that yard and make it look like you just won yard of the month.

If you have any budget for updating, your key areas to focus on are the kitchen first and then the bathrooms, and in particular, the master bathroom because that's your buyer's bathroom. Also, focus on the master bedroom as much as you can especially the closets. Master closets are so important.

Wherever you can invest any kind of money, be sure that it's very neutral and the design flow is consistent. Again, a quick staging consult could prove so beneficial in this situation as well. Keep in mind that you're putting a marketable product out there and it needs to be visually appealing to the vast majority of potential buyers.

Most importantly, you have to know who you're marketing to in your area, who your potential buyer is. That's who you want to focus on and to keep in mind when you're putting your updates in.

That's great information. Many people skip the important things and go for 'Let's make sure it's clean' and they think it's all that's needed.

What you do is remarkable. It's valuable and it also sounds like you probably have a lot of fun doing it.

What is it that led you to create this business that allows you to do your magic and help investors and homeowners sell their homes?

Rhonda Conchola: Well, I've always been interested and intrigued with the whole idea of home renovation and flipping houses. I've even done a couple of flips myself with my family.

I've also loved that home staging allows me the opportunity to express myself artistically. I've found that home staging marries the two concepts of me being able to express myself artistically, as well as being a part of the very strategic real estate world. I've found great fulfillment in having a part in helping others to accomplish their goals by showing a home's full potential. By adding that beautiful design conception that generates a quick sale.

I love what I do. It is fun, it's challenging and it's a lot of hard work. But it allows me, at the end of the day, to get that testimonial that says, "Thank you so much for helping me to sell my house quickly." Just being able to help people accomplish their goals is what gives me the most fulfillment. Because I know that's what I want for myself one day.

It's my passion. It's never work for me. It's something I love to do.

That's the secret right there, isn't it?

So how can people find out more about Rhonda Conchola and what you're doing and how to work with you?

Rhonda Conchola: They can go to my website, www.HomeStagingForHouston.com. They can also view my portfolio on my Houzz.com website at www.HomeStaging4Houston.com or call me at 832-301-5696 to set up a time to meet. I'd love to help out.

I am also on social media. Do a search for “Home Staging for Houston” in Facebook and you can like our business page. You can also see several photo samples of my work there. We specialize in working with real estate investors, so that’s our ideal client.

About Rhonda Conchola

As an innovative leader in home staging, Rhonda works with many design-savvy clients who have come to expect her simplistic yet pragmatic, sophisticated, yet refined approach to interior styling revealed in each project completed by Rhonda and her styling team. Known for bold color designs, memorable creativity and superior customer service, Rhonda offers a keen eye and the most cutting edge technology in home staging and interior styling.

Recently awarded Best of Houzz 2015, Rhonda is also a member of the Real Estate Staging Association and the Association of Property Scene Designers and regularly attends continuing education workshops to transform each project with the latest design styles and trends.

Outside her professional life, Rhonda enjoys quality time with her husband and 3 children, health and fitness, furniture restoration, and is actively involved in her home church praise team. She also enjoys dabbling with photography.

Business Name:	Home Staging for Houston
Website:	HomeStagingForHouston.com
Facebook:	Facebook.com/GetItStaged
LinkedIn:	LinkedIn.com/in/GetItStaged
Twitter:	Twitter.com/GetItStaged
YouTube:	YouTube.com/c/HomeStagingForHouston
Houzz.com:	HomeStaging4Houston.com

PROPERTY MANAGEMENT

C. Jerry Ta is a property manager with Propertycare, a rental property management company that helps landlords and investors step away from managing their investment properties.

Investors who hand over the day-to-day operations of property management to someone else can instead focus their time and resources on finding more deals, finding more money, making more money or simply having more quality time with their family.

Jerry discusses the mistakes that many first-time investors make when trying to handle their own property management and the many things involved in doing so. He also shares the services that his company provides to investors, no matter how many properties they may have, to allow them to enjoy the passive income they're generating.

Conversation with C. Jerry Ta

In your experience with managing rental properties, what is the number one mistake that people make when starting to build their rental property portfolio to build wealth and passive income?

C. Jerry Ta: I believe people go in with the right intentions and there are always people who lead you the right way initially. But then they let your hand go once you figure it out from there on.

Probably the first mistake a lot of investors make is they do not hire a real estate agent or some kind of leasing professional to identify a qualified tenant here when leasing out their properties.

You can easily rent out a property within one day in Houston, however, finding a good qualified tenant is the difficult part and it involves being able to advertise and market the property, find potential tenants, and properly screen the potential tenants.

A lot of investors do not want to pay a commission for leasing services and they try to take on that process on their own from the start and that is generally their first mistake.

When people are investing in rental properties, they have a romanticized vision of buying a few houses and renting them out. The tenants will pay down the mortgage and they get the rest as cash flow.

If you're screening tenants, what criteria do use to make sure that you have the right tenants in your houses?

C. Jerry Ta: To have the right tenants, you want to perform a good background check or screening on each potential tenant. There are two parts to it that I consider. The tenant must have the ability to pay rent and the willingness to pay rent, so we're referring to income and credit.

Do they have a good credit history? They may have the income, but they may not have the ability or willingness to always pay rent on time and that will hurt you.

In addition to receiving the applicant's paystubs, you will also need to call the employer and verify that the potential tenant actually works there currently.

I've come across situations where I've had fraudulent paystubs submitted, so I have been be a little more alert in that regard.

Yes, if they're going to misrepresent that, then they have no problem coming up with some evidence or false proof. So tenant selection is certainly a big piece of this.

Another thing is the lease agreement can be a pretty daunting piece of paperwork. In fact, it can be more paperwork than the actual purchase agreement.

C. Jerry Ta: I don't know the exact number of pages, but the lease agreement does have more pages than the purchase agreement. I believe the lease agreement is approximately sixteen pages versus a purchase agreement, which is approximately 9 pages.

Just like in a purchase agreement, there is a lot of legal language that protects both sides of the equation. As far as the Texas Real Estate contract goes, it does lay out a lot of different things, such as what amount to pay and when it's due. Texas is definitely a landlord state and there are a lot of protections in there for a landlord. In order to properly protect yourself, you must read through that lease agreement in detail and understand your responsibilities as well as the tenant's responsibilities.

You realize that there's no way someone can say this is a standard lease agreement because there are just so many variables in there, as far as what can and can't be.

Knowing how to fill those out correctly is almost a necessity to have a successful rental property.

C. Jerry Ta: Right. As far as the lease agreements that I use, I use the standard Texas one. There are variables or blanks to complete, but the template is setup in such a way that it does protect both parties.

One of those variables, for instance, is who pays for a repair?

Some landlords want the lease to state that the tenants have to pay the first $200 of a repair.

Some investors feel if you put that in the contract, you'll get a house back where nothing ever was repaired because the tenant is not going to pay for it.

C. Jerry Ta: Right. I do have a lot of landlords that request I put in the lease that the tenant is responsible for the initial $200 in repairs or a repair deductible. To your point, that's exactly what happens, the repairs are not made. If there's a leak under the sink, there may not be a reason why the tenant would want to fix it if it does not affect them. They could put a towel under there so it doesn't leak on the ground or something.

They're less likely to notify you of required repairs if they feel like they're going to be responsible to pay for it.

Right. Because essentially what you're doing when you do that is you're saying, "I want you to care about my investment as much as I do." And that just doesn't happen in the real world, does it?

So when people take on investment property, they come to realize very quickly that real estate can be an aggravation. A very profitable aggravation, but it can be an aggravation.

What does a management company provide to get people out of the day-to-day of dealing with those aggravations?

C. Jerry Ta: I just want to backtrack just a moment. As you were saying, a landlord gets a property and they think they'll rent it out. They receive rent. They pay down the mortgage. And they earn a little bit of cash flow.

In reality, once you lease the property, there are going to be additional repairs that are required, especially for older properties and that is usually a significant cost once you move away from the initial remodel or renovation of the property.

One of the days in the year that I receive the most phone calls is the first day in Houston when we have to turn on our air conditioning units. I get more than a dozen calls on that one single day from people that have air conditioning units that are either not working, not turning on correctly, or not cooling. A non-working air conditioning unit would be considered an emergency here in Houston.

For sure. And of course, heating is another issue.

What are some other big things that pop up in rental properties that can't be ignored?

C. Jerry Ta: I believe my number one calls for maintenance is for air conditioning here in Houston.

When I first started owning rental properties, one of my bigger obstacles was that I had a corporate daytime job. I worked in a cubicle and I was the only person fielding these maintenance calls. I would then have to find a contractor that could actually resolve the problem and be able to coordinate it in such a way where the issue is fixed.

To answer your question, that's what a property management company does. We facilitate in fielding those phone calls. We're that person that takes all the different phone calls and we make sure that we coordinate whichever contractor needs to be called to get the repair job completed.

You brought something that shows how property management can pay for itself. You work closely with different trades and have relationships with people that can fix the different issues.

It doesn't occur to people until they get that call that the A/C isn't working that the cost can be dramatic when they call an A/C repair company, compared to what you're been able to negotiate with trades and the people that you use in managing these properties.

C. Jerry Ta: Right. Because if you're just going to a retail company that does A/C, the repair cost will generally be higher. We do business with these companies almost on a daily basis, so we do get favorable treatment and cost reductions, at the same time.

When someone puts a property into a management agreement, how much involvement does the property owner have when issues come up?

C. Jerry Ta: Our goal is for the owner to have as little involvement as possible. It generally works better in that scenario. There are some owners that want to be heavily involved in the management and in those cases I'm not even sure I understand why they were needing a property manager.

The idea is for owners to trust that we'll take care of their investment and do the necessary repairs that we think are valid and reasonable. I think most owners understand that if the A/C is not working, there's no reason why a tenant would cause their A/C to not work or break it on purpose.

If the repairs are above a predetermined threshold and we're going to have to put a lot of capital expense into the property, that's when we actually involve the owner to make sure we get their approval.

For instance, if we're putting a brand new air conditioning unit into their property, we definitely want their approval beforehand. For minor maintenance requests and small repairs, we generally will go ahead and take care of those items. We do alert the owners and provide owner's statements and support for all repairs.

But the goal is for them to have trust in us in managing their investment.

Obviously, that is one of the big benefits of not having to deal with those midnight phone calls.

Now, when a tenant moves out or when it comes time for lease renewal, some people will raise the rent and don't care if the tenant moves out.

Other people say it's cheaper than the cost of doing a make ready and finding new tenants so they won't raise the rent.

What are your thoughts on that?

C. Jerry Ta: The official answer is that it depends. But for the most part, I generally do increase rent and I think you need to because your other expenses have increased. When I say other expenses, I'm referring to insurance and property taxes, those items.

Here in Houston, insurance premiums have generally increased year over year. The past couple of years, property taxes have also increased by a large margin at the same time.

So if you're not willing to increase the rent, you have to understand that your margin is decreasing annually.

How many tenants leave over a minor rent increase, versus those that are fine with it? Because all landlords have that fear that they're going to move out and it's going to cost a lot.

On the other side, are there tenants that feel it's worth paying an extra $25 or $50 versus the cost of having to move?

C. Jerry Ta: From my experience, if you're increasing at a reasonable rate, it has been easy to raise the rental rate. Keep in mind, when I provide these increases in rates, I also provide a reason behind it.

I believe tenants have an understanding of the costs and they look at the available rental properties around them and a lot of other rental properties have increased rates also. So if they're moving, it does not necessarily mean that they're moving into a better situation.

And as you said, it does cost quite a bit of money to actually move homes also.

So from my experience, as long as the rate increase is reasonable, and is still within market, the tenants are willing to accept that rate increase. I think everyone knows that insurance and property taxes have increased in Houston from year to year, so that conversation with tenants has been easier.

When the time comes, and it's inevitable for a lot of rental properties that a tenant does move out, a lot of times that causes a surprise to investors that haven't had that situation before.

When they first buy that property and renovate it, it's in pristine condition. How often does it actually come back to them in pristine condition?

C. Jerry Ta: Not very often. But, at the same time, we do hold a security deposit to repair the home for items that are beyond normal wear and tear on the property.

What you just said is important – wear and tear. They should never expect to get that property back in the exact same shape as when it was originally leased. Wear and tear is expected and acceptable to a certain degree.

What needs to be done to a property to be made ready for a new tenant, when the previous tenant was a good tenant and left it with normal wear and tear?

C. Jerry Ta: For one, if there's carpet in the home and the carpet is still usable and there are not major stains on the carpet, we always shampoo the carpet prior to a new tenant coming into the home.

There are always going to be minor scuffs on the wall. That's normal wear and tear. Usually a little bit of light paint touch-up. Almost everyone understands that. We also always hire a maid service to come through and clean the home.

When the tenant moves out, we either require them to hire a maid service or clean it themselves up to a certain standard. Or, we will deduct the amount to have the house cleaned from the security deposit and perform the work ourselves. We do the same thing with the carpet cleaning.

Many investors overspend on renovations up front, which can be costly when it comes time to do make readies when a tenant moves.

What are some of your recommendations to people that are coming in to do a renovation for a rental property, versus something that they want to sell or they want to flip, to make sure that that house is maintenance friendly?

C. Jerry Ta: As far as maintenance friendly, one of the things that I do, and I believe is pretty obvious, if you have multiple rental properties, you should use one color for the interior paint. That helps drive consistency across all properties.

I also limit the amount of carpet that is in the home. Generally, it's only limited to the bedrooms and their corresponding closet. I've seen many investors install carpet in the hallway leading into the bedrooms, which in my opinion is not a good idea. The hallway is a very high traffic area that links all the bedrooms together and may need to be replaced prior to the carpet in the bedrooms.

If you install tile or vinyl plank in the hallways leading into the bedrooms, you can replace carpet in individual bedrooms without having an impact to other bedrooms.

Depending on what class of rental property you have, I usually change the stairs if it's carpet; I put wood or some kind of hard surface on it. There is some additional cost, but you would never have to replace the carpet on the stairs again. And, again, that's a very high traffic area so I try to stay away from carpet in any and all high traffic areas.

Someone who owns one or two rental properties can have as much aggravation and headaches as someone that owns ten or twenty rental properties because your headaches don't necessarily grow in volume with the number of properties. Especially when you have a property management company.

When people are growing their portfolios, if they keep things cookie cutter, does that lower the maintenance and is it easier to manage that portfolio?

C. Jerry Ta: Yes it does and to your point, when you have ten, everything we do is systems and processed based. So if you're only doing one, you will generally not maintain a system or process in place. But when you're doing ten, you may have a process in place to gain some kind of efficiency.

As far as your clients, what is the range of how many single-family homes they may own?

C. Jerry Ta: I have a variety. I get accidental landlords every once in a while. This has happened more often than not when people get relocated for a job and they're not ready to sell a property they just recently purchased. Or, sometimes they receive a property from parents that have recently passed away.

Some clients are professional landlords, and they have more than twenty rental properties. They generally have their processes down pretty well, but there is still a large time commitment with it. That's when they start looking for a property manager to take that time commitment away from them.

Share the analogy you make with people who invest in rental properties and people who invest in things like stocks, bonds and mutual funds.

C. Jerry Ta: Whether it's a stock, mutual fund, bond or any kind of investment, there is always an asset manager in place that is managing that asset and the day-to-day functions of it.

When an owner or landlord purchases the rental property, he purchases an asset. At that point in time, he's really become an asset manager of his own investment. What investors do not realize is that there's a significant time commitment that comes along with owning the asset. From finding the tenant to setting up the lease agreements, and finding quality and reliable contractors to do work if there is remodeling or renovations required at the property.

When you start reallocating your time to managing your investment property, it is time taken away from other activities that you may have had with family, hobbies, or whatever else.

That really brings the value to what a property manager can do. Without putting a dollar value on it, we're talking about the value of your time.

What are some of the criteria people should look for when they're trying to choose the right property manager for their rental portfolio?

C. Jerry Ta: One of the things to consider is whether the property manager actually has rental properties of their own. If they have never been in your shoes, as far as being an investor or a landlord, it would be difficult for them to understand the perspective of an investor or a landlord.

So I believe having multiple rental properties is important, as well as their experience in areas geographically. There are certain suburbs of Houston that I will not manage just because I do not have experience in that area or I do not possess enough resources in that area to manage a property correctly.

It's not just about being able to answer calls and manage repairs. It's about understanding the business of being a landlord.

One of the dirty words out there that a lot of landlords, and people that are thinking of being landlords, are afraid of is "evictions." You hear nightmare stories about bad tenants or tenants that won't move or won't pay rent.

What are the myths versus the facts in Texas around evictions? How often do you actually have to go through that eviction process?

C. Jerry Ta: How often you have evictions may very well depend on how well you screen the tenant. If you screen your tenant very well, and they have a good income source, a good employment history, a good rental history, and a good credit history, you will generally be faced with fewer problems in the future.

If you start making exceptions with regards to all these criteria, then you will more likely to have to go through an eviction.

When I hear property managers say they do lots of evictions, my response or thought is that they're probably not screening the tenants properly or well enough.

Granted, you're still going to get some here and there. But it should never be a lot.

So if you're diligent up front and go through the steps that you talked about when choosing the right tenants, then a lot of times, that can be avoided.

Does the property management company actually start the eviction process and file the paperwork on behalf of the landlord?

C. Jerry Ta: Yes. We file the notice to vacate and will file the eviction with the court. If necessary, we will also make the court appearance for the landlord.

So it's almost a done for you process that takes a lot of the stress off the landlord from trying to understand the actual process.

Something else people seem to be unclear about is security deposits. What are some things landlords should know about a security deposit? And what's the amount of security deposit that you recommend at a minimum for people that are taking on tenants?

C. Jerry Ta: The security deposit should at a minimum be equal to one full month's rent. Generally, I will ask for more than one full month's rent.

Recently, for people with lower credits scores due to isolated credit issues, but have excellent income, I have requested a double deposit in order to place them in the rental property.

When it's time for the tenant to move out, how do you determine how much of that security deposit a tenant will get back?

C. Jerry Ta: We go through the process of inspecting the house. Security deposits are held as separate trust accounts and untouched until the day the tenant moves out. It's only meant to cover damages to the home beyond normal wear and tear and for any unpaid charges to the tenant.

When you say normal wear and tear, what does that cover?

C. Jerry Ta: We require tenants to shampoo the carpets after they move out or we'll take care of that process for them. We bill them or we reduce it from the security deposit. The reason for that is usually either we provide them with brand new carpet, or we clean the carpets right before they move in. So the expectation is for them to return the property in the same condition that we provided it to them, less wear and tear.

We understand there will be small stains here and there that can't be removed. But for the most part, it should be relatively clean and maybe just trafficked a little bit.

You talked about the security deposit being held in a separate account. Is that part of the law or part of the contract that that's held separately so that it's there and it doesn't get spent or have any questions about it at all?

C. Jerry Ta: It is required by Texas property code that the security deposit is held in a separate trust account.

What about pets? Do you recommend that people allow pets and charge more of a deposit? Are there things that you warn people about, as far as legal or liability issues with that?

C. Jerry Ta: We normally do allow pets, but we do not allow any type of dangerous breeds, such as pit-bulls, Dobermans, German Shepherds.

Under Texas Pet Agreement contract, there are three items that we can charge a tenant for to allow them to have pets. First, there is an additional security deposit related to pet damages. Second, there can be a non-refundable pet fee charged up front before the tenant moves in. Third, there can be an increase in rent that can be charged.

So these are the little nuances that a property manager is going to help people navigate through.

The benefits of property management are pretty obvious. Good property management is going to more than pay for itself by getting a house leased quickly, understanding the market, and understanding how to screen good tenants.

If someone just got their first house and they're thinking they may not be ready for a property manager, what should they do to prepare for the many facets of property management? Or is having just one property still a good candidate for having a property manager?

C. Jerry Ta: You know, I've actually had quite a few people with just one property. I had previously mentioned before that a lot of people become landlords by accident. In those situations, they may not want to deal with the tenant and do not want to be a landlord at all.

It just made sense for them. They wanted the cash flow but they did not want the headaches that came along with it.

Again, there are certain tasks that you're going to have to do if you want to self-manage the property. Getting the property rent ready, market the property, find a tenant, leasing it to the tenant, as well as repairs and collecting rent after the property is leased.

Even if it's just one property, it will take time away from other parts of your lives during the day.

If you have a client that has accidentally become a landlord, do you offer advice with renting the property?

C. Jerry Ta: Oh, yes, definitely. We talk to many different people in different situations all the time. We try to see what makes sense for them to help them make the decision as far as if they should rent the property or not.

The price ranges for rental properties in Houston are wide.

Where do you see that sweet spot for success for people that are running profitable landlord portfolios?

C. Jerry Ta: In Houston, it just depends from neighborhood to neighborhood. I hate to state a general rule on it, but if you go from one neighborhood to the next, one street to the next, the market could really change.

So the answer is it could be great in one neighborhood and you move one street over and it may not be great anymore. You really have to evaluate every home in every neighborhood, based on where it's located.

That is what you do and what you're very good at. We are really thrilled and privileged to have you as part of this Houston Real Estate Investor's Dream Team.

How can people find out more about you and your Propertycare management services?

C. Jerry Ta: Anyone can go to my website, www.propertycarehouston.com or reach me on my office phone. I also regularly attend and available at various real estate networking events in throughout Houston.

About C. Jerry Ta

C. Jerry Ta is a Houston, Texas based real estate agent, investor, and property manager. He is the founder and managing partner of Propertycare LLC, a Houston-based property management company and is also the owner and operator of a successful Houston-based HomeVestors® franchise. Mr. Ta has been involved in real estate investment since 2011 and owns and operates a portfolio of rental properties across the greater Houston area.

Prior to his work in real estate, he served as an as an external auditor for Ernst & Young and PricewaterhouseCoopers as well as an internal auditor for a large oil and gas corporation. In his work as an auditor, he performed full scope audits of financial statements for large SEC and non-SEC clients, including companies in the global 500 and multinationals.

Mr. Ta is both a licensed Certified Public Accountant (CPA) and licensed Real Estate agent in the State of Texas. Formal education includes a Bachelor of Business Administration (BBA) degree from the University of Houston (2005) and a Master of Science in Accountancy (MSA) degree from the University of Houston (2006).

Mr. Ta lives in Houston with his wife, Kim Do Ta. The couple wed in 2009.

Business Name:	Propertycare, LLC
Website:	www.PropertycareHouston.com
Facebook:	Facebook.com/propertycarehouston
Twitter:	Twitter.com/PropertycareHTX
YouTube:	YouTube.com/user/PropertycareHouston
Google+:	Plus.Google.com/u/0/+Propertycarehouston

BOOKKEEPING FOR REAL ESTATE INVESTORS

As a former accountant, Thuy T. Vo is an expert with numbers, to the benefit of Houston real estate investors. Currently a bookkeeper, Thuy works exclusively with real estate investors, as she helps to simplify and handle the drudgery of keeping track of the extensive financial information involved in keeping the IRS at bay at the end of the year.

Many in the real estate industry are not aware of the bookkeeping nuances and differences involved in the real estate worlds of landlording versus flipping properties or fixing them to see for retail.

In this chapter, Thuy discusses how she helps those in the real estate investing world maintain the financial records they need in order to stay in compliance with the tax laws and also save money when these records are handed over to an accountant. She shares how to organize, streamline and manage accurate bookkeeping records.

Conversation with Thuy T. Vo

Bookkeeping is a word that can send chills down people's spines.

What is the first thing that someone needs to do when you help investors with organizing, streamlining and managing their bookkeeping for their real estate business?

Thuy T. Vo: When I first sit and talk with my clients, there are a few things I need to know. How big is their business? What are they doing? Is it all rentals? Is it all rehabs? By understanding where they are with their business and where they want to go, I can provide some kind of structure.

But at a minimum, they need to have records. It can be as simple as a spreadsheet that keeps track of all the transactions. All the ins and outs.

Then even if they don't have a bookkeeper, they can take the history of all the transactions and all the expenses to the accountant or CPA at the end of the year and give that accountant a lot to work with.

You talk about taking information to the accountant at the end of the year. Explain the difference between a real estate investor bookkeeper's job versus the real estate investor accountant's job.

Thuy T. Vo: As a bookkeeper, maintaining records is an ongoing weekly or monthly task. You can have a lot of transactions from every time you pay a bill or pay a contractor. The bookkeeper's job is to keep all the receipts and expenses categorized in the way that follows the accountant's principles.

We categorize all expenses, direct and indirect and capitalize what has to be capitalized, and it makes the accountant's job a lot easier. We give them the whole picture for the year. Everything is summarized and categorized the way that they need it and this will save the investor a lot of money.

We've learned in this book that there is a big difference between holding rental properties, doing rehabs and flips, and doing wholesaling when it comes to the way to do your taxes. One of the biggest dangers is to intermingle those businesses and those records.

What are some of the things that people need to think about when they're actually categorizing expenses for their real estate transactions and all the things that they do in their real estate business?

Thuy T. Vo: There is a misconception where people think that bookkeeping for real estate is just like any bookkeeping. It's not. The transactions and the principles of things are different.

When you purchase a rental property, there are some expenses that cannot be expensed that year. You cannot expense it until you fix up the property and it's ready and made available for rent.

For a rehab, it's the same thing. If you're buying a property with the intention of fixing it up and selling it, you cannot expense anything until the property is sold. All your costs are the basis of the property.

Knowing that can make a difference in the taxes planning for the year.

Let's say you have two different investors. One person is a landlord and is going to rent a house. Another person is buying and flipping houses.

If they have houses right next door to each other in the same neighborhood and they both need to get new roofs and new air conditioners, would their books look the same?

Thuy T. Vo: Let's say Property A is a rental and we have to spend money to put on a new roof and put in a new A/C. This is considered an improvement and it is subject to depreciation rules. The new roof and A/C are considered part of the property and will be depreciable over the life of the property (27.5 or 39 years). So in year that the expense occurred, only a small portion can be deducted.

However, you cannot expense anything with Property B that you're fixing up to sell. Let's say you start doing that rehab in May and you spend $5,000 for a new roof, $5,000 for a new A/C and $5,000 for a foundation. All of that is added to your cost. It cannot be expensed until you sell the property.

If you did not get the house ready until January of the following year, you have zero expense for the current year. You cannot deduct any of the expenses that you put into the house. All of that are categorized as capital expenditures. When you sell the property in January of the next year, your purchase costs, your improvement costs and all your holding costs would be your cost of goods sold.

So it's a big difference. But some investors are thinking if they spend the money, they should be able to deduct it in the year it occurred.

That's one of those misconceptions people have because there are considerable expenses to doing real estate ventures and they don't discuss these tax implications on the flipping houses shows.

If an investor is renting out a house, they can start the process of taking a partial deduction as soon as that house is ready to put on the market for rent. If they put a sign in the yard in December, then they can start deducting in December, whether or not someone has actually leased it or not.

Is that correct?

Thuy T. Vo: Correct. As soon as the house is ready and made available for rent, yes, then it is a rental. Then you can start deducting part of the expenses depending on the type of the improvement. Is it a 5-year property? Then you can depreciate it over five years. And if it is a 7-years property, you spread your depreciation deduction over seven years.

Knowing all these principles can make a huge difference in your bottom line at the end of the year. You can determine when to put the house on the market. Do you need to expense this year or will that expense make a difference next year?

Knowing how the principles work, you can use that to your advantage and ultimately keep more money in your pocket.

Let's talk about contractors and sub-contractors. If you hire people, do you have to give them a 1099 or do you write it down as an expense?

What are some of the mistakes real estate investors make when they're hiring contractors?

Thuy T. Vo: I always try to educate my clients as to what their responsibility are as somebody who hire contractors or sub-contractors.

By law, when we pay somebody within the year at least $600, we must give them a 1099, whether they want it or not. I have clients tell me their contractors don't want it. It's not what they want – the company that hires them is responsible for collecting their 1099 information and reporting their earnings to the IRS by February 28th.

As long as we take care of it and give them the 1099 and report the earnings to the IRS, we fulfill the requirement.

What are the consequences of not doing that? Are you going to end up having that as a non-qualified expense, where you're going to pay the taxes on that as income yourself?

Thuy T. Vo: Well, you are talking about two different things here. Yes, there are consequences for not reporting the 1099 earnings to the IRS. The penalties can be as high as $200 for each unreported 1099. But you are not going to end up with non-qualified expense.

At the end of the year, if we did pay that expense, we can deduct it. The problem arrives when you get audit, and the IRS finds out that you paid a contractor $1,000 and there was no 1099 reported, you will get penalized.

Well, that's really important because a lot of times, people think a light bulb is a light bulb. But when it comes time for bookkeeping and taxes, that light bulb can be classified in many different ways.

Some real estate investors have a book and they write down everything they spend. They deduct the total amount spent from their income and think that's what they owe taxes on. It's not that simple, is it?

Thuy T. Vo: No, it's not that simple. For most businesses, what comes in is income and what goes out are expenses. But it doesn't work like that with real estate investing.

With the example we were talking about previously with the rental and the flip, what can be expensed this year and what cannot be expensed is different. So every time they pay something, we need to know exactly which property was it for and what's the purpose or strategy for that property?

It's so important to know what the client has in mind for the outcome for that property because everything gets recorded differently.

That is a very important term – the intent of that property.

Let's say someone has a property that they want to rent and they get it ready for rental. They put the sign in the yard to rent in November and they do all their taxes at the end of the year. But then in January, the house hasn't rented and somebody comes by, offers to buy it and they end up selling it.

Talk about the bookkeeping and going back and restructuring things based on intent, versus what may actually happen because in the real world, plans change.

Thuy T. Vo: Well, in the example that you just mentioned, there's not much of an impact as far as what I need to do as a bookkeeper because I keep each property separately. There's no commingling between property A and B, so the numbers are clear for every property at any given time.

When the intention changes and they say, "Okay, we no longer want to keep it as a rental. We're now selling it," it's just a matter of me moving that property from one category to the other.

Before they sell or before they rent, I still have it as an inventory item so it's easy for me to move and re-categorize the property at any time. And in this business, this is typical.

I have come up with these structures so I can manage all of this very easily by keeping things very clear and having everything separate for each property.

Clarity is something that is hard to find sometimes, especially when people start building their portfolio and have a number of properties.

They may get caught up in the day-to-day spending of money and don't keep an accurate picture of what's really costing them money and where there might a leak in their expenses.

Talk about that clarity and the importance of a Profit and Loss statement, something where people can easily look at a snapshot of their business.

Thuy T. Vo: What just came to mind is a conversation I had not so long ago with one of my clients. He became my client seven months ago and it took us a while to get all the records straight.

When that was done, I showed him his Profit and Loss by project because I have it for each property. It's something he'd never seen before and we had an amazing conversation.

He has a number of rentals. Now the market is doing pretty well and he's thinking about selling one or two. I was looking at the numbers and I said, "Do you want to see which one is making money for you. And what is your goal? Do you want $300 from each property? Do you want $500 from each property? So looking at it, which one is making you money and which one is sucking the money from you?"

And he said, "Oh, my God. I never looked at it that way." I told him this would help him choose which one to sell.

That's the kind of clarity I bring to my clients. I give them many ways to look at where they are in their business and they can make powerful decisions based on the information at hands.

So he said he could see which property was not making money for him and it was very easy for him to choose which one he was going to fix up and sell.

That's an incredibly powerful decision, especially, when rentals are between tenants. Maybe there is a decision to be made on how much should be put into a house to rent it again, versus should the property be sold.

How often should people be looking at that snapshot of their business?

Thuy T. Vo: It should be a monthly thing. Because it's very important to know where you are. As an active investor who is constantly buying and selling and making decisions, you need to know where you are. You also need to know where your bottom line is, as well as what you're coming out with at the end of the year, and whether you're in the positive or in the negative. Then you can plan your path.

Another thing a lot of people don't know is to keep track of depreciation. I have clients come to me and say they never care about that. I tell them if you don't take advantage of the depreciation, you've lost it. That's a big deal. The IRS says that you had it and you didn't take it. Too bad.

So when they determine whether to sell a house or not, knowing the depreciation recap is a big deal.

If you buy a property for $100,000 and you've been depreciating the value of the home for, let's say, 15 years, what is the tax implications of selling that home? It's so important to know.

Does it make sense to sell that house today? Will you come out ahead knowing that you're going to have to recapture all the depreciation expenses and what's the tax implication of that transaction? Will it make a difference if you sell a year later when you have more losses or more income?

Having all that information is very powerful because you can make effective decisions that ultimately will keep more money in your pocket.

Many entrepreneurs and real estate investors do what could be called checkbook accounting. Their budget is based on what they have in the bank. "Can I do this marketing? Well, yes, the money's in the bank. I can do the marketing."

How important are those snapshots for not just seeing where you are, but also being able to project what you can do and actually see trouble coming around the horizon?

Also, how important is it to be able to look at historical data in order to make certain projections and budgets for things such as marketing or vacancies?

Thuy T. Vo: It's very important. I always tell my clients, "It doesn't matter how smart you are. Knowing where you are financially, where the money is and how much is going in and out every month, and where your overhead expenses are is important because if you don't know that, you're going in blindly and that's no way to be successful."

Many of my clients who do a lot more volume have offices and we will do cash flow projections to see where they are. We find out how much they need to come in every month just to maintain the office and keep the payroll going. So there's no guessing. It's bring clarity to everything that they do and all the decisions they make.

That definitely helps not just their business and finances, but it probably helps people sleep at night.

How important is it for real estate investors to keep separate bank accounts for purchasing things that are for their personal life versus purchasing things strictly for the business?

Thuy T. Vo: It's very important. A lot of people think that it has to be complicated but it doesn't need to be. If you're not incorporated, or maybe doing business as a DBA, or you don't have a separate name, just have a separate checking account. Maybe put aside one of your credit cards and just use that one credit card to make purchases for business.

It's hard for us to keep track of all the receipts. But it's simple to pull the statement. As a bookkeeper, I go from the source. I work with the source that is the statement. By doing that, you are guaranteed not to miss any expenses. If you're going to have to write a check, just write a check from one checking account. If you need to use your credit card, just use that one.

A lot of people don't realize that it's not even about having to go and set up a company and business bank account. Even if they set up a separate personal bank account and set aside a Master Card they haven't been putting expenses on and use those exclusively for the real estate business, that's good enough.

Thuy T. Vo: Yes. It doesn't have to be complicated. That's good enough.

The thing is if you're going to mix business with your personal accounts, it just causes a lot more trouble later down the line and it's a lot more work to keep track of.

Ultimately, commingling accounts will cost more money. Either you're going to need to have a bookkeeper that spends more time seeking out which one is what, or if you don't have a bookkeeper, your CPA will have to do that. And it's going to cost a lot more time.

But the worst thing is when you get audited, then the auditors are going to look into everything in your personal business. And it doesn't have to happen that way.

Yes, that is an incredibly important distinction.

What are those important things that people should look for when seeking a bookkeeper so that they can make sure that bookkeeper understands the subtleties and nuances of the real estate business?

Thuy T. Vo: Well, it's a big difference when it comes to real estate investing. A bookkeeper for a real estate investor cannot be just any bookkeeper. It has to a bookkeeper that know how to handle the different types of transactions in real estate business.

You also need to find a bookkeeper that understands creative transactions.

Obviously, a bookkeeper comes with an expense and people don't want to hire a bookkeeper because they think that's an expense that they don't need.

But smart investors that come to you as clients very quickly realize that you aren't an expense. You're actually making them money or saving them money, rather than costing them money.

What would you say to help investors realize that a bookkeeper is not something they're spending money on, but rather it's something that is helping them to increase their bottom line and helping them avoid financial problems?

Thuy T. Vo: If people are looking to get into real estate investing as a hobby, then yes, you can manage your own books.

But if people are serious about doing it as a business and making big money, then a very important aspect of the business is to have a bookkeeper that knows real estate business because that will ultimately put more money in their pocket.

Right. Because one wrong move could cost you thousands, if not tens of thousands of dollars.

Thuy T. Vo: Correct. It's one of the investments that will bring them so much more at the end of the year. We can manage the books and bring integrity to the books. But in addition, we know the expenses that they can take and we tell people what else they can do to minimize the taxes at the end of the year.

So I think when people bring on the right bookkeeper, it will automatically help increase their profits and not their expenses.

You're not just a bookkeeper for real estate investors, you're a real estate investor yourself.

What is it that actually led you to create this business, to be a bookkeeper for real estate investors and to really focus on that and work exclusively with investors?

Thuy T. Vo: Well, I never thought this is what I would be doing. I worked as an accountant for eleven years. When I moved to Houston, I was sure that's not what I wanted to be doing. I didn't want to start another full-time job. I wanted to make more money. I wanted financial freedom. I wanted more time.

That's when I started looking into real estate and started investing. I did that for a couple of years and I did some flips. I also did owner financing and got very creative.

I needed to find an expert in taxes and how to handle those, and that's when I met Michael Plaks. When I got to know Michael and he got to know about my background and what I used to do, he was the one that asked if I would take on some of his client projects and help them with their books.

Throughout my eleven years as an accountant, I always had a side business of bookkeeping for small businesses. But it was more like a hobby. I just wanted to help them out. They knew that I did accounting.

Michael said, "You already know Quick Books and you know real estate. Why don't you do this?"

So I started helping out with some projects and he kept telling me I had something so valuable. He said I could create a good business doing this but I wasn't sure I wanted to do this.

After I took on more projects for Michael, I saw the difference I made and I saw the value I brought to those clients. The service I could do didn't seem to exist out there. I think it's because of my background in accounting. I know Quick Books. I know bookkeeping. And I love real estate.

From 2010 to 2014, I went to many seminars and events to learn about real estate here in Houston. I have learned a lot and I bring a lot of that to my clients. The more projects I take on for Michael, the more I love it. It's like a seed that I can mold.

So that's how my bookkeeping business was founded. I really love what I'm doing, and for me, it's not about the money. It's about the difference I make and the contribution I bring to all these businesses.

It's an incredible place to be where I can talk real estate and then do my bookkeeping and bring the knowledge I have in accounting. So it's a very unique service that I bring to my clients.

It is and it is certainly one that is so incredibly important and yet so often neglected by a lot of people that get into real estate.

How can people find out more about you and your business, if they want to get involved?

Thuy T. Vo: To find out more, they can visit my website, at www.REIBookkeeper.com.

About Thuy T. Vo

Growing up, Thuy T. Vo dreamed of becoming an Math teacher. But, in 1989 after coming to America with her family, she realized financial independence was the necessary ingredient to be successful. And she did not think a teaching career would get her there.

In college, she majored in Business with a concentration in Accounting since she was good at math. Thuy began working part-time as a bookkeeper for a small business handling the account receivables and payables processes while attending college. In 1999, she graduated from Montclair State University in Upper Montclair, NJ with a BS in Accounting. She then took on a full time job working for one of the Fortune 500 companies.

Thuy enjoyed her job and was promoted four times in the first seven years. The last position she held was as the Accounting Manager managing 10 employees. She knew that she had come a long way and was perceived as being successful. However, she felt a void and felt trapped. She was neither happy nor satisfied with her career path.

In 2008, Thuy and her husband moved to Houston from New Jersey to be closer to family members. She wanted to jumpstart on a new career. She became interested in the real estate business after attending several seminars. She joined various real estate clubs in Houston.

The career change was stressful but Thuy was determined not to have to go back to corporate America. She was the youngest of six siblings and the only one to finish High School and college. Her career change was met with little support from family and friends.

Still, she pursued real estate investing. Thuy did her first flip in early 2011 after meeting Brant Phillips, who was the contractor hired to do her first project. She went on to do several flips that included owner financing, wholesale deals, and a couple subject-to deals.

Real estate bookkeeping happened by chance. Thuy was looking into creative financing options for her projects and needed a tax accountant who was an expert in this field. She hired Michael Plaks to handle her taxes. Once Michael learned about her background, he asked if she was interested in doing some real estate bookkeeping.

She was hesitant at first as wanted to focus on her real estate projects, but agreed to take on some projects. Since then, several clients have been referred to her through other investors.

Through this business, she found it again...that incredible satisfaction in making a difference and making a contribution to her clients' businesses. Thuy's accounting background, knowledge in taxation and her passion for real estate investing has enabled her bookkeeping services to be unique and different.

When people hire REI Bookkeeper to take care of their books, not only do they get professional, affordable services but they also get a partner in their real estate business – a partner who has their best interests at heart.

Business Name: REI Bookkeeper

Website: REIBookkeeper.com

Made in the USA
San Bernardino, CA
19 July 2017